The Cosmic Conflict

Between Christ and Satan

John M. Fowler

Pacific Press® Publishing Association
Nampa, Idaho
Oshawa, Ontario, Canada
www.pacificpress.com

Edited by Jerry D. Thomas
Designed by Dennis Ferree
Cover art © Justinen Creative Group

Copyright © 2001 by
Pacific Press® Publishing Association
Printed in the United States of America
All Rights Reserved

Additional copies of this book may be purchased at
http://www.adventistbookcenter.com

Unless otherwise indicated, all Scripture quotations are from The New
King James Version.

Library of Congress Cataloging-in-Publication Data:

ISBN 0-8163-1867-0

01 02 03 04 05 • 5 4 3 2 1

Contents

Dedication

To Mary
my friend and life companion of forty years,
who taught me so much as to how to walk this journey of faith
in the conflict of the great controversy.

Preface

I was thirteen and not yet a Seventh-day Adventist. On the sidewalk near my high school in India, the used bookseller had spread his wares. A set of five books caught my attention. Beautifully bound, they were priced only five rupees (at that time, about $1). For the son of a miner, even that was too much. I struck a bargain at four rupees and brought them home. Thus began my introduction to one of the marvelous commentaries on redemptive history. I was particularly fascinated with the author's persistent theme of this great fight between God and Satan. I finished the last few gripping chapters of *The Great Controversy* in one sitting. My life would never be the same.

Later when I became a Seventh-day Adventist, that theme became the integrating factor of my life and studies in Adventist college and seminary. That theme provided a worldview. It gave me a ground to stand upon. After forty-two years of ministry in the Church, the theme still holds a grandeur, provides a hope, and defines a destiny—at least for me.

In the writing of this book, those books were extremely helpful. What would we do without them and others that flowed from that inspired author?

The theme of the great controversy can in no way be exhausted. I would only suggest for readers a better and a greater way: go to the Bible, go to the Spirit of Prophecy, study, and pray. Taste and see what the Lord has in store.

Introduction

I phoned her, but Jenny did not answer. Three times that summer morning I tried, only to learn that she was not well.

Just a headache, a bit of dizziness, I was told, and she would be back at her desk in the morning. But the following day she wasn't there. It was unusual for Jenny to lie in bed just from a headache. Was it something more serious? Before the final diagnosis was in, she was gone. All within two weeks.

Jenny was a child of God. No other words can aptly describe her. She had a profound conviction that her life was meant for the service of God and her fellow humans. She believed and lived the gospel. Every phase of the Christian faith had a vital bearing on her life and she had committed all her resources to the witness of that faith.

Four days before her death she sat in the front row at church for a youth service. She was in pain, but she didn't want to miss either fellowship or worship. Three days before her final hour she had a long season of prayer with a valued friend. Both women prayed, poured their hearts out to God, affirmed their faith in God's will and grace, and sought for that divine power that alone makes living purposeful.

Jenny's prayer, I am told by this friend, was selfless. Not a single word did she utter on her own behalf. She did not plead for her pain to be removed. She did not cry for healing or for health or even for the life that was hanging on by such a slender thread. Instead, she prayed that God's will would be done. She prayed for Winfred, Janice, Maxine, and other young people in the community that they would all be within the embracing arms of a loving Father.

She prayed that she too would remain in that embrace.

And suddenly she was gone. Young, believing, exemplary child of God.

Why? Where was God when Jenny died?

The problem of suffering and death has ever been a part of the human story. Every age, every culture, every person has wrestled with the mystery of pain. Why does an earthquake in a moment of fury swallow up thousands of innocent people? Why does war bring out the worst in human pride and arrogance, leaving in its path millions of dead and destitute? Why does a tornado sweep away whole villages and towns? Why does a cell multiply unhindered, leading to that dreadful diagnosis of cancer? Why does hatred and prejudice create walls of division and bitterness between people on account of color, ethnicity, caste, or economic disparity, leading to senseless tragedy, denying the dignity of humanity, and defying the Creator's demand of love as the basic principle of living?

That Why? is the perpetual question of history.

Many answers have been given; many solutions offered.

To an atheist, neither the personal suffering of Jenny nor the genocide of an entire people poses a philosophical problem. Tragedy just happens to be so—face it if you can, accept it if you must, but don't ask any questions about meaning or purpose in life. Life is to be lived as best as one can make it; technology may bring some hope for a better life; science may promise a cure for what is incurable now; history may teach that suffering is no stranger to the present. The roaring sea, the quaking earth, the plummeting plane, the invasion of a disease all just happens. Don't look for any special meaning, for there is no such meaning. There is no God who can enter human life and provide clarity in the midst of chaos.

To others, suffering is a result of *karma*—the unalterable law of fate. The grief of a young widow, the humiliation of an outcast, the mutilated body of a leper, the wasting system of an AIDS victim, the destruction of an entire city—all these are merited results for the misdeeds of a former life. The only way to escape suffering is to do the maximum good in the present life, hoping for a better deal in the next life. Such hope knows no end, for life is an endless cycle of existence and extinction.

To still others, suffering is a result of *kismat*—the decree of God. He misleads whom He will, and whom He will He guides. This being so, nothing happens without the consent of God.

Accept it and keep going.

The answer from the Bible

The answer from the Bible is quite different—in fact, radically different. While it does not deny the reality of suffering, it does not attribute it to God. The Scriptures present God:

As good and just. "Good and upright is the Lord" (Psalm 25:8). "Oh, taste and see that the Lord is good; blessed is the man who trusts in Him!" (Psalm 34:8).

As loving, kind, and merciful. " 'For the mountains shall depart and the hills be removed, but My kindness shall not depart from you, nor shall My covenant of peace be removed,' says the Lord, who has mercy on you" (Isaiah 54:10).

As One who eases suffering. "I led them with cords of compassion, with the bands of love, and I became to them as one who eases the yoke of their jaws, and I bent down to them and fed them" (Hosea 11:4, RSV).

As a tower of strength to those in trouble. "The Lord is good, a stronghold in the day of trouble; and He knows those who trust in Him" (Nahum 1:7).

Nowhere is the certainty of God's love and goodness better illustrated than in the life and teachings of Jesus. Whatever Jesus did, He did out of love. The sight of a disfigured leper (Mark 1:41), the funeral procession of a widow's only son (Luke 7:13), the groping of a blind man (Mark 10:49), the sight of hungry multitudes (Matthew 14:14)—these moved the heart of the Master. Certainly He was "touched with the feeling of our infirmities" (Hebrews 4:15, KJV).

Christ brought a new dimension to the understanding of the character of God. As against the notion that God is some sort of a vengeful, impersonal cosmic judge, indifferent to human feelings, Jesus presented God as the heavenly Father, supremely interested in the well-being of His creatures. He cares for the fallen sparrow. His ears are open to the cry of distress. He loves. He listens. He heals. He helps. He leads. He forgives. He saves.

Introduction

If God is such, who, then, is responsible for the predicament we humans are in? Who is responsible for countless afflictions that plague human community?

Jesus Himself has provided the answer. In the parable of the weeds (Matthew 13:24-30), Jesus speaks of a farmer who sowed good seeds in the garden. When the plants came, the farmer's servants noticed many weeds growing along with the wheat, and they asked, "Sir, did you not sow good seed in your field? How then does it have tares?" Jesus' reply is significant: "An enemy has done this."

The enemy is none other than Satan. When Jesus saw a woman crippled for eighteen years, He described her as one bound by Satan (Luke 13:16). Paul, too, saw the enemy at work when he referred to his ailment as "a messenger of Satan" (2 Corinthians 12:7).

That Satan is responsible for suffering is clearly established in the first few chapters of the Bible. In the beginning, says the scripture, God created a perfect world. No hunter stalked his prey. No fragrant blossom withered and died. No sickness, no sorrow, no death, plagued the life of our first parents—until Satan entered.

With cunningness turned into craft, with rebellion given the flavor of freedom, with death portrayed as life, the adversary confronted Adam and Eve. The first parents fell to the temptation. They preferred the delusion of Satan to the declaration of God. They trusted the enemy and disbelieved the Creator. They broke their relationship with God.

At once humanity came under the curse of sin. " 'Cursed is the ground for your sake; in toil you shall eat of it all the days of your life. Both thorns and thistles it shall bring forth for you, and you shall eat the herb of the field. In the sweat of your face you shall eat bread till you return to the ground, for out of it you were taken; for dust you are, and to dust you shall return' " (Genesis 3:17-19).

Thus we see that the origin of suffering and death is not in the plan of God but in the chaos brought about by sin. Everything sin touched withered, suffered, and died. "The whole creation groans and labors with birth pangs together until now" (Romans 8:22).

As long as sin is in the world there will be suffering. As long as the adversary is at work, there will be pain. We cannot run away from heartaches. We cannot evade the slings and the arrows. We cannot deny the

9

reality of death. But we can turn to the biblical portrayal of history in order to find understanding and meaning as to why evil exists and what its end will be.

That portrayal of history dominates the Scriptures from its opening pages to its closing climax under the unifying motif of the cosmic conflict between God and Satan, between good and evil, between truth and falsehood. Seventh-day Adventists have called this motif the great controversy, and have included it as one of their 27 Fundamental Beliefs. The belief, as described below, forms the framework of the study of this book:

"All humanity is now involved in a great controversy between Christ and Satan regarding the character of God, His law, and His sovereignty over the universe. This conflict originated in heaven when a created being, endowed with freedom of choice, in self-exaltation became Satan, God's adversary, and led into rebellion a portion of the angels. He introduced the spirit of rebellion into this world when he led Adam and Eve into sin. This human sin resulted in the distortion of the image of God in humanity, the disordering of the created world, and its eventual devastation at the time of the worldwide flood. Observed by the whole creation, this world became the arena of the universal conflict, out of which the God of love will ultimately be vindicated."*

---

*Seventh-day Adventist Church Manual, chap. 2, p. 9.

CHAPTER

War
in Heaven

T here was war in heaven" (Revelation 12:7, KJV).

The very phrase "war in heaven" seems like a paradox. The word "heaven" evokes all that is good, perfect, joyful, and harmonious. Heaven is where God's throne is (Isaiah 66:1), and thus it is the symbol of God's sovereignty over all creation. As His dwelling place, and as the center of His divine and moral authority, heaven can be conceived only as a place where absolute goodness, righteousness, love, and perfection dwell. Nothing evil can mar the perfection of heaven. Nothing contrary to God's character can make its abode in heaven.

Genesis 1 speaks about a creation that was "very good." At the end of each day of creation God pronounced that it was good, and on the final day He said that the entire creation was very good (Genesis 1:4, 10, 12, 18, 21, 25, 31). What is applicable to earthly creation is equally valid to the entire cosmos. If God had made the earth good and created human beings without any evil, how much more so is His perfect creation of heaven and heavenly beings.

And yet the Bible describes that "there was war in heaven." The word "war" indicates that there arose in heaven something or someone contrary to God's will. That someone questioned God's role in the created order, His character, and sovereignty. Such rebellion cannot exist in heaven, and it needed to be dealt with. Hence, there was war in heaven: Michael and his angels fought against the dragon; and the dragon fought and his angels, and prevailed not; neither was their place found any more in heaven. And the great dragon was cast out, that old serpent, called the Devil, and Satan, which deceiveth the whole world: he was cast out into the earth, and his angels were cast out with him (Revelation 12:7-9, KJV).

Two sides in the war

Revelation explains the war in heaven as one that took place between Michael and Satan. Revelation 12:10 describes the victory in this war as won by Christ. From this and other passages in the Bible (Jude 9; Daniel 10:13, 21; 12:1), we can conclude that Michael is a name attributed to none other than Christ.

The name Michael as the name of a heavenly being appears in the Bible only in apocalyptic passages (Dan. 10:13, 21; 12:1; Jude 9; Rev. 12:7), in instances where Christ is in direct conflict with Satan. The name in Hebrew, signifying "who is like God?" is at once a question and a challenge. In view of the fact that Satan's rebellion is essentially an attempt to install himself on the throne of God and "be like the most High" (Isa. 14:14), the name Michael is a most fitting one for Him who has undertaken to vindicate the character of God and disprove Satan's claims.[1]

The great controversy is thus a cosmic conflict between Christ and Satan. But the question is: If God is perfect and has created a universe without any flaw or tendency toward evil, how did sin originate in heaven? How did a being like Satan rise in the midst of such a perfect place as heaven? The origin of rebellion against God is a mystery.

It is impossible to explain the origin of sin so as to give a reason for its existence. Yet enough may be understood concerning both the origin and the final disposition of sin to make fully manifest the justice and benevolence of God in all His dealings with evil. Nothing is more plainly taught in Scripture than that God was in no wise responsible for the entrance of sin; that there was no arbitrary withdrawal of divine grace, no deficiency in the divine government, that gave occasion for the uprising of rebellion. Sin is an intruder, for whose presence no reason can be given.[2]

Even though the reason for the entrance of rebellion in heaven cannot be fully understood, there are sufficient clues in the Scriptures as to what led Satan to become the leader of the rebellion in heaven.

First, consider the analogy of Adam and Eve, and their fall into sin. Satan led Adam and Eve to sin by telling them that God had withheld from them something that they could easily have if they only followed him. If they could only eat the forbidden fruit, they could become like God (Genesis 3:5). Between the Creator and the creature, there is a line that ought not to be crossed. Satan's temptation to our first parents was precisely this: cross the forbidden line. The result was the entrance of sin, a rebellious state against God.

To assume the authority of Christ as the Creator, to be like the Son of God, was the cherished ambition of Satan in heaven. With a creature wanting to become the Creator, he sowed the seeds of discord in heaven. Just as he tempted our foreparents, he held the fruit of becoming like God before the angels and misled a third of them. Eventually, God had to deal with this rebellion and hence war in heaven began.

Second, Jude 6 suggests that the fallen angels "did not keep their proper domain, but left their own habitation." Add to this Paul's warning that no recent convert should be appointed a bishop lest he be "puffed up with pride" and "fall into the same condemnation as the devil" (1 Timothy 3:6), you get the picture that the sin of the fallen angel was dissatisfaction with his status and a desire to become like God. The angelic sin, therefore, is a desire to cross the boundaries of creaturehood and become like the Creator.

Third, the passage that describes war in heaven depicts Satan as " 'the accuser of our brethren, who accused them before our God day and night' " (Revelation 12:10). What was Satan's accusation of the "brethren" before God? Verse 11 provides a fascinating insight. Satan's charge before God is His sovereign role as the Redeemer of the lost human race. The victory in the great controversy as Revelation 12 portrays is the victory won by the blood of the Lamb (v. 11). Satan's contention is that God cannot be holy and just, and yet save the sinful human race. In so charging, Satan refused to acknowledge that God's character is one of infinite love. An angelic being in the presence of God chose to question God's love and justice—something that Satan continues to do among the human race even today. If God is loving, why all this suffering? If God is loving, why should death be the lot of humanity?

Little by little Satan spread his dissatisfaction about God's character among angels, leading to a revolt. How God chose to handle this conflict is in itself a lesson in love.

The covering cherub

Two passages that describe Lucifer's sin dramatically deserve to be noted. Both are in the Old Testament. The first one is Ezekiel 28:12-17. Guided by the Holy Spirit, Ezekiel uses the figure of the king of Tyre, an evil and morally bankrupt monarch, to portray the king of all evil. "The first sinner was one whom God had greatly exalted. He is represented under the figure of the prince of Tyrus flourishing in might and magnificence."[3]

Ezekiel begins his description by saying that Satan was not created evil. He was created good and appointed as the "anointed cherub." " 'You were perfect in your ways from the day you were created' " (Ezekiel 28:15).

The anointed cherub describes the lofty position of responsibility God had given to this angelic being. In spite of his office, " 'iniquity was found in' " Lucifer (Ezekiel 28:15). What was his iniquity? Verse 17 states: " 'Your heart was lifted up . . . you corrupted your wisdom.' " Instead of acknowledging God as the Source of all that he had, Lucifer looked to himself, and in a spirit of pride and self-sufficiency, he chose to place himself against the Creator. "Sin originated in self-seeking. Lucifer, the covering cherub, desired to be first in heaven."[4] There began the seed of revolt.

Lucifer's sin

Ezekiel uses the king of Tyre, and Isaiah uses the king of Babylon (Isaiah 14:12-15) as representative of the king of all evil, and from these passages we can understand the origin and nature of Satan, his character, and his revolt. Just as God was behind David's throne (Isaiah 41:20; Zephaniah 3:15), Satan was behind the throne of the evil monarchs of these pagan kingdoms. Just as David was to reflect God's character, so the kings of Tyre and Babylon, in a way, reflect the characteristics of Satan.

Isaiah applies the title "Lucifer" to describe the position Satan once held as leader of angels in heaven. The Revised Standard Version translates "Lucifer" as "Day Star." Christ is also referred to as "the day star" (2 Peter 1:19, KJV), " 'the Bright and Morning Star' " (Revelation 22:16). Applied to Satan before his fall, the term reflects the high position he once held in heaven—that of leadership of angels. But a creature's position is always lower than that of the Creator who is the Christ (John 1:1-3; Ephesians 3:9; Hebrews 1:1-3)—a factor that Lucifer refused to acknowledge.

That refusal made itself open in the throne room of God, amidst the presence of angels, by Lucifer's making some claims that are utterly intolerable and unacceptable. Note a few of these claims recorded in Isaiah 14:13-14:

" ' "*I will ascend into heaven, I will exalt my throne above the stars of God,*" ' " claimed Lucifer. Lucifer's ultimate presumption is that he can usurp the sovereignty of God, and claim a throne above all thrones. The claim is based on the false notion that a created being can become the Creator. Scripture often calls us to practice a spirit of humility, and to have the mind of Jesus, who practiced ultimate humility by taking upon Himself the form of a servant and died upon the cross (Philippians 2:2-5). What a contrast between the spirit of Lucifer and the spirit of Jesus.

" ' "*I will also sit on the mount of the congregation on the farthest sides of the north,*" ' " said Lucifer. Psalm 48:2 describes Mount Zion as being "on the sides of the north." This mount of the congregation is a spiritual symbol that God alone is the Sovereign of the cosmos, and that He alone is worthy of all worship, praise, and allegiance from His creatures. Lucifer's claim and search is that he should be the object of worship. Worship is God's sole prerogative from all creatures. That prerogative is based on His being the Sovereign Creator and Redeemer. Lucifer's attempt to assume that he, too, can be worshiped was a challenge that God could ignore and yet remain God. Hence, Lucifer had to be dealt with as a rebel who should be cast out of heaven.

" ' "*I will ascend above the heights of the clouds, I will be like the Most High,*" ' " boasted Lucifer. To be like God, to love like Him, to serve like Him, to forgive like Him—all these are Godlike characteristics that we as creatures must ever seek. But this was not the aim of Lucifer in seeking to be like God. Power and position, not love and service, characterized Lucifer's motivation. Such claims on the part of Lucifer and those who chose to follow him led to the rebellion in heaven. Eventually, God had to cast them out of His sacred abode.

Satan cast out of heaven

Was there anything that God could have done to prevent Satan from being thrown out? God is a God of love, and He relates to all His creatures out of that love. The Bible does not provide us details of what God did with the rebellious angels before they were thrown out. But from the way He deals with erring sinners here on earth, we can be sure that His plea for repentance, His offer of forgiveness, and His readiness to accept the repentant ones would not have been any less with Lucifer than with us. "A compassionate Creator, in yearning pity for Lucifer and his followers, was seeking to draw them back from the abyss of ruin into which they were about to plunge. But His mercy was misinterpreted."[5] Lucifer claimed that God's longsuffering was a show of weakness, that God would give in if the rebellious angels stood firm.

And so the adversary rejected every plea of a loving God and plunged the created order into a cosmic conflict between him and God. Once that was done, the controversy had to be played out to the end to reveal to the universe the true nature of God and the true motive of the rebel. That God is just and loving, holy and perfect, and in whose presence no rebellion can thrive needs to be shown, and the great controversy would take its time and course and ultimately triumph in the victory of God over Satan—His justice and love over Satan's rebellion and sin.

Another question arises: Since God is Almighty and All-Powerful, why did He not crush the rebellion at its start?

Even when he was cast out of heaven, Infinite Wisdom did not destroy Satan. Since only the service of love can be acceptable to God, the allegiance of His creatures must rest upon a conviction of His justice and benevolence. The inhabitants of heaven and of the worlds, being unprepared to comprehend the nature or consequences of sin, could not then have seen the justice of God in the destruction of Satan. Had he been immediately blotted out of existence, some would have served God from fear rather than from love. The influence of the deceiver would not have been fully destroyed, nor would the spirit of rebellion have been utterly eradicated. For the good of the entire universe through ceaseless ages, he must more fully develop his principles, that his charges against the divine government might be seen in their true light by all created beings, and that the justice and mercy of God and the immutability of His law might be forever placed beyond all question.[6]

Still another question: why did God not force the rebels to return to the faithful fold? One of God's gifts to humans is freedom of choice (Deuteronomy 30:19; Joshua 24:15). God gave the same gift to the angels as well. While He does not want forced obedience, can He be held responsible for the result of disobedience on the part of His creatures?

"The law of love being the foundation of the government of God, the happiness of all created beings depended upon their perfect accord with its great principles of righteousness. God desires from all His creatures the service of love—homage that springs from an intelligent appreciation of His character. He takes no pleasure in a forced allegiance, and to all He grants freedom of will, that they may render Him voluntary service."[7]

Exercising his own freedom of choice and establishing himself and his followers in their rebellion against God, Lucifer crossed the point of no return. And in the ensuing war, so graphically portrayed in Revelation 12, Satan and his followers were cast out of heaven.

"In the banishment of Satan from heaven, God declared His justice and maintained honor of His throne. . . . The mighty argument of the cross demonstrates to the whole universe that the course of sin which Lucifer had chosen was in no wise chargeable upon the government of God."[8]

---

1. *Seventh-day Adventist Bible Commentary* (Washington, D.C.: Review and Herald Pub. Assn., 1955) 4:860.
2. *The Great Controversy,* pp. 492-493.
3. White, *Seventh-day Adventist Bible Commentary,* 4:1162.
4. *The Desire of Ages,* p. 21.
5. *Patriarchs and Prophets,* p. 39.
6. *Ibid.,* p. 42
7. *The Great Controversy,* p. 493.
8. *Ibid.,* pp. 500, 501.

CHAPTER 2

Issues in the Cosmic Conflict

What are the issues that sparked the great controversy between God and Satan in heaven?

Although no one biblical passage speaks directly on this subject, we may safely conclude from the overall biblical portrayal of the conflict that at the basis of the controversy is the character of God and how He relates to the created order. What makes God God? Is He a personal being, full of love and compassion? Or is He a despot, demanding from His creatures absolute obedience and surrender? What is the basis of His operation in the universe? Is He just and fair in expecting obedience to His law and allegiance to Him as the Creator and Redeemer? Can He be just and still be loving and merciful? What is the role of Christ, the Second Person of the Godhead, in God's plan and government?

These are some of the great questions at the center of the great controversy. As we review these issues, we need to keep in mind our limitations. God is infinite; we are finite. God is eternal; we are frail. God is omniscient; we are dependent upon His revelation for what little we know. Mortals that we are, we are approaching a divine mystery when we study the issues in the cosmic conflict. God is holy—absolutely holy—and we need to put aside our shoes as we approach this study in which God has risked everything—including His Son in the process of incarnation.

God's moral law

Revelation 12:17 concludes the narration of the war between Christ and Satan by stating that Satan was "enraged with the woman [the true church], and he went to make war with the rest of her offspring, who keep the commandments of God."

If Satan's war with the people of God is because they are faithful to God's law, it can be safely inferred that one of the primary issues in the great controversy in heaven was the law of God. Further, the Scripture says: "The devil has sinned from the beginning" (1 John 3:8), and it defines sin as: "Whosoever committeth sin transgresseth also the law: for sin is the transgression of the law" (1 John 3:4, KJV).

Because Satan has sinned from the beginning, and because sin is the transgression of God's law, it is obvious that Lucifer questioned in heaven the necessity of obedience to God's law and argued with his fellow angels that God's law is arbitrary and unjust.

But sin is more than transgression of the law. It is rebellion against God. In his magnificent prayer Daniel confessed Israel's sin as an act of rebellion: " 'We have sinned and committed iniquity, we have done wickedly and rebelled, even by departing from Your precepts and Your judgments' " (Daniel 9:5). Likewise, David describes his own sin as an affront to the character and person of God (Psalm 51:4). So when Satan is described as one who sinned from the beginning, it is clear that sin not only had its origin in Satan, but that it is an act of defiance and rebellion against God, and a transgression of His law and His will.

Lucifer's claim, " ' "I will be like the Most High" ' " (Isaiah 14:14), is a further indication that Satan chose to rebel against God. Satan

> had sought to falsify the word of God and had misrepresented His plan of government before the angels, claiming that God was not just in laying laws and rules upon the inhabitants of heaven; that in requiring submission and obedience from His creatures, He was seeking merely the exaltation of Himself.[1]

But the opposite is really the truth. God's requirement for moral uprightness and obedience to His law arise not from God's selfishness, but His desire that His creatures be partakers of His character and be like Him: holy, righteous, and loving. Because God is holy, He demands His creatures to be holy, but that life of holiness is not based on any subjective feelings. It must be based on an objective, divine norm. That norm is God's moral law. It is "a transcript of His own character, and it is the standard of all character. This infinite standard is presented to all that there may be no mistake in regard to the kind of people whom God will have to compose His kingdom."[2]

In accusing that the law of God was arbitrary, Satan was attacking the very foundation of God's government and character. Every government requires certain laws for it to function smoothly and effectively. It may be that an evil government may have laws that are not just and fair, but God's government, by the very nature of His character of holiness and righteousness, cannot be evil. Goodness, righteousness, and holiness are the essential nature of God, and His law, therefore, cannot but be "holy and just and good" (Romans 7:12).

If Satan began the revolt in heaven by rebelling against God's law, consider the attitude of Christ concerning the law. In His incarnate status, on God's mission to crush Satan (Genesis 3:15) and assure the triumph of God in the great controversy, what a positive attitude Jesus took regarding the law of God! Even before Jesus was born, the Messianic prophecy of Psalm 40:8 declared of Him, " 'I delight to do Your will, O my God, and Your law is within my heart.' " His teaching regarding the law was one of establishing its permanence:

> "Do not think that I have come to abolish the Law or the Prophets; I have not come to abolish them but to fulfill them. I tell you the truth, until heaven and earth disappear, not the smallest letter, not the least stroke of a pen, will by any means disappear from the Law until everything is accomplished" (Matthew 5:17, 18, NIV).

His life was consistent with His teaching, and He kept the law whereby He abode in God's love (John 15:10). He lived a sinless life and His life is a testimony against Satan's charge that the law is impossible to be kept.

Indeed Satan's charge against God's law was taken so seriously by the Creator that God risked His Son's life in sending Him in human flesh. The life, ministry, the cross, and the resurrection of Jesus stand as eternal mileposts that declare to the universe that God's law is not arbitrary and that it is the unchangeable standard of God's government. It was so in heaven. It is so now on earth. And it shall be so for eternity.

> The warfare against God's law, which was begun in heaven, will be continued until the end of time. Every man will be tested. Obedience or disobedience is the question to be decided by the whole world. All will be called to choose between the law of God and the laws of men. Here the dividing line will be drawn. There will be but two classes. Every character will be fully developed; and all will show whether they have chosen the side of loyalty or that of rebellion.
> Then the end will come. God will vindicate His law and deliver His people. Satan and all who have joined him in rebellion will be cut off. Sin and sinners will perish, root and branch (Mal. 4:1),—Satan the root, and his followers the branches.[3]

God's love and authority

One of the most descriptive passages regarding the character of God is 1 John 4:8: "God is love." Throughout the Scriptures we find the love of God described as an essential divine quality that defines His relationship with humans. The New Testament word often used for God's "love" is *agape.* The word denotes love in its highest, fullest, and most selfless sense. The theme of the entire Bible is the self-revelation of the God of love, and it reaches its height when God sent His Son to redeem the sinners. Everything God does—His law, grace, mercy, providence, and even judgment—flows from love.

Even God's law is a result of His love. Jesus gave the fullest expression to this connection between God's law and love when He paraphrased the demands of the law in terms of visible behavior. When a Pharisee asked Him as to which is the great commandment,

> Jesus said to him, " 'You shall love the Lord your God with all your heart, with all your soul, and with all your mind.' This is the first and great commandment. And the second is like it: 'You shall love your neighbor as yourself.' On these two commandments hang all the Law and the Prophets" (Matthew 22:37-40).

"The law of love being the foundation of the government of God, the happiness of all intelligent beings depends upon their perfect accord with its great principles of righteousness. God desires from all His creatures the service of love—service that springs from an appreciation of His character."[4]

If God is love, what was Satan's charge in the great controversy? Could it be that Satan was covertly advocating among his cohorts that God's relationship with His creatures is not based on love, but on His selfish desire to be supreme and His arbitrary way of forcing allegiance of all creatures to His will and way? Could it be that Satan was jealous of the position of Christ as coequal with God in creating and governing the cosmos that he spread the lie that if God was truly loving to all His creatures, He could not be favoring Christ by letting Him share His throne?

Jesus described Satan as a liar and a murderer from the beginning—even before the creation of Adam and Eve (John 8:44). In what way was he a liar? What was his murder about? The lie of Satan is his persistent denial that God is love, and he continues in that lie even today. The murder that Satan indulged in was his attempt to falsely represent God's character and his continual attempt to usurp Christ's authority.

> Instead of seeking to make God supreme in the affections and allegiance of all created beings, it was his endeavor to secure their service and loyalty to himself. And coveting the glory with which the infinite Father had invested His Son, this prince of angels aspired to power that was the prerogative of Christ alone....
>
> God Himself had established the order of heaven; and in departing from it, Lucifer would dishonor his Maker and bring ruin upon himself.[5]

So to disprove Satan's charge that God's love is not genuine, God sent His Son to this world to show that He loved sinful humanity so much that He was ready to sacrifice the life of His Son in order to reveal His love and reconcile the world unto Himself.

> Satan led men to conceive of God as a being whose chief attribute is stern justice,—one who is a severe judge, a harsh,

exacting creditor. He pictured the Creator as a being who is watching with jealous eye to discern the errors and mistakes of men, that He may visit judgments upon them. It was to remove this dark shadow, by revealing to the world the infinite love of God, that Jesus came to live among men.[6]

God's Son

What was Satan's dispute regarding Christ? The onslaught of Satan against Jesus in the wilderness temptations provide us some understanding. The first two temptations were prefaced with a call to self-doubt: "If you are the Son of God ..."

> The Son of God shared the Father's throne, and the glory of the eternal, self-existent One encircled both ... none but Christ, the Only Begotten of God, could fully enter into His purposes, and to Him it was committed to execute the mighty counsels of His will.[7]

Christ knew all this, and yet in His moment of weakness after forty days of fasting, the tempter casts the bait of self-doubt. Satan failed to accept Christ's preeminent position as the Coequal of the Father, but Christ refused to entertain any self-doubt on this score—not in heaven, not on earth. Nor would He employ His divine power to satisfy His own needs.

Another of Satan's disputes regarding Christ had to do with Christ's prerogatives of worship and Creatorship. Isaiah's portrayal of Lucifer (Isaiah 14:12-14) includes his persistent seeking for himself worship that only God deserves. That was in heaven. On earth he went to the extreme of tempting Jesus to worship him in exchange for all the kingdoms of the world (Matthew 4:8-10). Implied in this temptation is Satan's claim that he is the lord of the earth, and he had the authority to do whatever he wished. He was claiming both ownership and lordship of this earth—something he was seeking in heaven as part of his revolt, and now on earth brazenly assuming to be true. But Jesus denounced Satan for what he was: a liar from the beginning. He rejected Satan and his claims: " 'Away with you, Satan! For it is written, "You shall worship the Lord your God, and Him only you shall serve" ' " (Matthew 4:10).

Satan falsely claimed ownership of this earth. True ownership belonged only to the Creator, and hence to Jesus, for He is the Creator of the universe. Thus, Satan's dispute concerning Christ was His preeminent position as the Creator of the world. For Satan fully knew that "if Christ made all things, He existed before all things.... Christ was God essentially, and in the highest sense. He was with God from all eternity."[8] Hence Satan disputed Christ's Creatorship and accused God as being partial toward the Second Person of the Godhead. "To dispute the supremacy of the Son of God, thus impeaching the wisdom and love of the Creator, had become the purpose of this prince of angels [Lucifer]."[9]

Only He in whom is life "original, unborrowed, underived"[10] can be the Creator. No creature such as Lucifer, however exalted and mighty, can be the Creator; for he himself owes his life and existence to God. But that was not the case with the Son. He is God and "all things were made through Him, and without Him nothing was made that was made" (John 1:3). But Lucifer became jealous that the Son, not he, was included in God's creative activity, and vowed that he will exalt his " ' "throne above the stars of God" ' " and that he will be like the Most High (Isaiah 14:13, 14).

The third temptation provides another area in which Satan disputed with God. Jesus' mission was to win back the lost earth and humanity for the Father by shedding His blood. The Cross was in God's plan of redemption before the foundation of the earth was laid (Revelation 13:8). Sending His Son to this earth, letting Him show that it is possible to obey God's law, and finally dying for the sins of the world was God's way of showing to the universe that He is both just and loving. But now in the wilderness Satan was offering Jesus a crown without the Cross, the world back to Him without having to climb Golgotha. Satan was offering Jesus a way counter to the way of the Father, and if only Jesus could be tempted to accept Satan's short-cut, Satan would have triumphed. To accept Satan's way was "to yield the victory in the great controversy. It was in seeking to exalt himself above the Son of God that Satan had sinned in heaven. Should he prevail now, it would be the triumph of rebellion."[11]

Thus it was, both in heaven and on earth, Satan put on his battle gear to defeat Christ in the great controversy. But the victory of Jesus was complete, and He can say to the Father: " 'I have glorified You on the earth. I have finished the work which You have given Me to do' " (John 17:4).

God's justice and mercy

Satan is a liar. He is a murderer. As if those descriptions are not enough, we have another pointed descriptive about Satan:

> Then I heard a loud voice saying in heaven, "Now salvation, and strength, and the kingdom of our God, and the power of His Christ have come, for the accuser of our brethren, who accused them before our God day and night, has been cast down" (Revelation 12:10).

What was Satan's accusation before God day and night? The context suggests that Satan cannot accept the fact that God's love has finally won out, and salvation and the kingdom of God has been fully realized by the power of Christ. Satan's accusation has always been the same: Can God be just and loving and merciful enough to forgive the sinner? If God expects obedience, then the God of holiness must meet out justice to those who disobey. Lucifer's argument: Grace is unfair. Justice demands death, and like Shylock's pound of flesh, Satan demands that death must be meted out to all those who disobey. But here is where God's love steps in. " 'For God so loved the world that He gave His only begotten Son, that whoever believes in Him should not perish but have everlasting life. For God did not send His Son into the world to condemn the world, but that the world through Him might be saved' " (John 3:16,17).

The initiative of God's love to save sinners is often called the act of God's grace. Satan knows the meaning of neither love nor grace. But to God love and grace are real and costly, just as justice is real and unchangeable. God's choice of dealing with sin through the manifestation of His grace cost the life of His Son. Who can estimate the value of that act of divine love? Gethsemane and the Cross, the dreadful wrath of God against sin witnessed there, show not only divine abhorrence of sin, but also the divine cost to effect the plan of salvation and to uphold the cause of divine justice. When Paul speaks of "God, who through Christ reconciled us to himself" (2 Corinthians 5:18, RSV), He is putting the Father and the Son together in the act of salvation, and shows that both paid a great price for making redemption possible. Grace did cost God a great deal, but in the process the divine plan showed that love and justice can exist in the heart of the Eternal One.

"By His life and His death, Christ proved that God's justice did not destroy His mercy, but that sin could be forgiven, and that the law is righteous, and can be perfectly obeyed. Satan's charges were refuted. God had given man unmistakable evidence of His love."[12]

Martin Luther dreamed he was standing before the judgment seat of God where Satan spread out a long scroll on which he had kept a careful record of Luther's innumerable sins. With great fervor, the accuser argued before God, "This man cannot enter the kingdom. He has violated the law times without number. He deserves death." Martin Luther then told Satan to take his hand off the scroll. Satan said, "I will not." Luther again demanded that he do so, and the devil again refused. Finally, Luther shouted, "In the name of Jesus Christ, move your hand." Satan then moved it from the scroll, where against his sins, it was written, "The blood of Jesus Christ cleanses Martin Luther from all his sins."

There lies the mystery of the Cross—how God lets His grace meet the demands of justice in the person of Jesus.

Thus, all the issues in the great controversy are nothing but full-blown fruits of self-centeredness. Whenever self proclaims itself as god, whenever a creature questions the role of the Creator in its life and destiny, whenever the love and the law of God are questioned in order to exalt self-indulgence, we have the great controversy at work. And nothing delights the author of the cosmic conflict more.

---

1. *The Great Controversy,* p. 498.
2. *Christ's Object Lessons,* p. 315.
3. *The Desire of Ages,* p. 763.
4. *Patriarchs and Prophets,* p. 34.
5. *Ibid.,* pp. 35, 36.
6. *Steps to Christ,* p. 11.
7. *Patriarchs and Prophets,* p. 36.
8. *Selected Messages,* 1:247.
9. *Patriarchs and Prophets,* p. 36.
10. *The Desire of Ages,* p. 530.
11. *The Desire of Ages,* p. 129.
12. *Ibid.,* p. 762.

CHAPTER

Contenders
in the Conflict

The war in heaven led to the expulsion of Satan and his followers to this earth. As we shall see in the next chapter, with Satan coming to this earth, he brought the cosmic conflict to this newly created world and turned it into a battlefield where he hoped he might disprove God's claims and become the ruler of this world. If he could not own this earth by obtaining the power of creation, he would do so by deceiving the earth's inhabitants and turning them against God.

But God's infinite wisdom did not leave this earth an unguarded prey for Satan. Even before the foundation of this earth was laid, even as the plans for creating the human race were completed in the heavenly courts, God had a plan to meet the contingency of such an event as Satan turning this earth into his battlefield. God would not leave humanity without a proper understanding of the controversy and without a means of deliverance from the clutches of the evil one. The apostle speaks of this eternal plan in these poignant words: "He [Christ] indeed was foreordained before the foundation of the world, but was manifest in these last times for you who through Him believe in God, who raised Him from the dead and gave Him glory, so that your faith and hope are in God" (1 Peter 1:20-21).

Divine love had conceived a plan whereby man might be redeemed. The broken law of God demanded the life of the sinner. In all the universe there was but one who could, in behalf of man, satisfy its claims. Since the divine law is as sacred as God Himself, only one equal with God could make atonement for its transgression. None but Christ could redeem fallen man from the curse of the law and bring him again into harmony with Heaven. Christ would take upon Himself the guilt and shame of sin—sin so offensive to a holy God that it must separate the Father and His Son. Christ would reach to the depths of misery to rescue the ruined race.[1]

"When the fullness of the time had come, God sent forth His Son, born of a woman, born under the law, to redeem those who were under the law, that we might receive the adoption as sons" (Galatians 4:4, 5). The incarnation of Christ, taking upon Himself human flesh, was God's chosen method to crush Satan and his rebellion and win the victory in the great controversy. Even though the Incarnation itself came about "in the fullness of time" according to God's great redemptive calendar, Christ contended with Satan over every battle for the human soul on this earth ever since Satan entered this world to seize it as his battlefield. The divine promise of Genesis 3:15 clearly indicates that Satan's work on earth will be countered by Christ from the beginning until the devil is finally crushed.

Thus the chief contenders in the great controversy are Christ and Satan. Christ as the Second Person of the Godhead is leading the forces of good against Satan and his allies. By contrasting Christ and Satan—who they are and what they do—we can understand better how focused the great controversy is on the character of God as it relates to His created order. Everything that Christ is or does is related to vindicating the character of God and rescuing the fallen race from the clutches of the evil one. Everything Satan does pulls the human race away from God's love and mercy.

These diametrically opposed motivations and methods between the two contenders become clear as we view the contrasting portrayals of them found in the Bible. One is God with us ready to save us, the other a roaring lion out to destroy us. One is the Lord of light, the other the prince of darkness. One is the God of truth, the other the father of lies. One is the Christ, the other antichrist. One is the Shepherd that cares for the flock, the other a wolf out to devour God's people. A study of these contrasts will help us focus on the triumph that awaits those who put their trust in Christ.

God with us vs. lion in our midst

Long before Christ took the human flesh in order to redeem the sinful human race and thus defeat Satan's plan in the great controversy, the prophet Isaiah, under the inspiration of the Holy Spirit, described His status: " 'Behold, the virgin shall conceive and bear a Son, and shall call His name Immanuel' " (Isaiah 7:14). Immanuel is also the name the New Testament applies to Christ whose main mission will be to " 'save His people from their sins' " (Matthew 1:20-22).

Immanuel means "God with us." Christ has always been God. And yet He left the glories of heaven and came down to this earth to accomplish Heaven's purpose in the great controversy. He became God with us, and as such became God's surety that those who accept Him and follow Him " 'should not perish but have everlasting life' " (John 3:16).

> By coming to dwell with us, Jesus was to reveal God both to men and to angels. He was the Word of God,—God's thought made audible. In His prayer for His disciples He says, "I have declared unto them Thy name,"—"merciful and gracious, long-suffering, and abundant in goodness and truth,"—"that the love wherewith Thou hast loved Me may be in them, and I in them." But not alone for His earthborn children was this revelation given. Our little world is the lesson book of the universe.[2]

On this lesson book is written in bold letters of crimson red that Christ came to be one of us, bear the burdens of sin, and die on the cross for our sins. In that substitutionary death, through the shed blood of Christ, God has "[reconciled] the world to Himself" and made us "the righteousness of God in Him" (2 Corinthians 5:19-20).

The apostle Paul who so gloriously writes of the peace that Christ has brought between the fallen and sinful human race and their Creator also raises a grand and awful question: "If God is for us, who can be against us?" (Romans 8:31).

The answer should be obvious. No one. Not on earth, not in heaven. Well that's the assurance Paul holds forth in the verses that follow the question, but for that assurance there is a condition: continual abiding in Christ and continual allegiance to God as the Creator and Redeemer. But the great controversy is not that simple. We are in a battle. As C. S. Lewis points out, "There is no neutral ground in the universe: every square inch, every split second, is claimed by God and counterclaimed by Satan."[3]

Since the deception in Eden, Satan always pretends to be a friend of the human race. He "frequently appears as an angel of light, assuming friendly airs, presenting peculiar temptations which it is difficult for the inexperienced to withstand. Sometimes he accomplishes his purpose of deluding the unwary by exciting the pity of their sympathetic natures, and presenting himself before them as a righteous being who has been persecuted without a cause."[4]

However subtle he may be, Satan remains our "adversary," "who walks about like a roaring lion, seeking whom he may devour." No lion waits for its prey to come to him. It has to be on its prowl, silently, stealthily, until it finds its feed. Likewise, Satan roams, night and day, cunningly to catch his victim. The allurement of this world, the pleasures of the flesh, the seeming goodness in what the eye can see, the ear can hear, and the heart can throb after, the illusions of what may seem as spiritual, and the promise of a great destiny at no cost are just some of the ways in which Satan may attempt to catch us unawares. As he did with Christ in the wilderness, Satan may also use self-doubt, self-satisfaction, a kingdom without the Cross, doubt in God's Word and promises, and questions regarding the claims of God as Creator and Redeemer in his attempt to "devour" the saints.

Peter should know what he was talking about. At one moment, he obeyed the Spirit of God and declared Jesus to be the Son of God; in the very next moment he became the agent of Satan and denied the way of the Cross (Matthew 16:13-16). At one moment, he expressed his readiness to die with and for Jesus; at the very next, he denied thrice he ever knew his Master (Matthew 26:35, 69-75). At one moment he rejoiced that in Jesus all walls of partition among people have been broken; at another he withdrew from the Gentiles (Acts 10:27; Galatians 2:11,12).

Satan attacked Peter often and desired to have him. Jesus knew this too, and assured him, " 'I have prayed for you, that your faith should not fail; and when you have returned to Me, strengthen your brethren' " (Luke 22:32).

Who of us has not been under attack from Satan? The attack is not the issue, for that is Satan's dedicated task. But do we know our safety, our refuge? Peter provides the answer:

"Resist him, steadfast in the faith" (1 Peter 5:9). And Paul adds: "Thanks be to God, who gives us the victory through our Lord Jesus Christ" (1 Corinthians 15:57). Under the banner of Prince Immanuel, we can experience victory in the conflict over sin and the roaring lion.

The Lord of light vs. the prince of darkness

Another biblical portrait of the contenders in the great controversy places them in the absolute contrast between light and darkness. Jesus said of Himself: " 'I am the light of the world. He who follows Me shall not walk in darkness, but have the light of life' " (John 8:12). John describes Jesus: "In Him was life, and the life was the light of men. And the light shines in the darkness, and the darkness did not comprehend it" (John 1:4, 5).

What an astonishing claim to make! Light of the world. Light that brought life. In all the annals of human history great men and women have come and gone. Buddha believed he had a marvelous message for humanity, but for himself he claimed nothing but a re-discoverer and searcher after truth. Krishna, as courageous and beneficent as he was, considered himself only a teacher of truth. Confucius dared not claim holiness or love but only the right to walk with others where he might find truth. Mohammed, great and lofty as he was, looked to God's cloak of mercy to find hope. But Jesus makes this audacious claim that He is the Light, and He was fully aware of what He meant. Those who follow Him shall not be in darkness but walk under the glorious sunshine of God's love and life. Indeed they will have the "light of life."

There is something absolute about God and Christ being Light: in them there is "no darkness at all" (1 John 1:5). Just as light is opposed to darkness, so is Christ opposed to the prince of darkness, Satan. As the presence of light dispels darkness, so the coming of Christ assures the defeat of Satan.

What does Satan do as the prince of darkness? Just what He did as Lucifer in heaven. He misrepresents the character of God, makes His law seem irrelevant, and casts doubts on God's self-disclosure in the Bible and through Jesus.

> The same spirit that prompted rebellion in heaven still in-spires rebellion on earth. Satan has continued with men the same policy which he pursued with the angels. His spirit now reigns in the children of disobedience. Like him they seek to break down the restraints of the law of God and promise men liberty through transgression of its precepts. Reproof of sin still arouses the spirit of hatred and resistance. When God's messages of warning are brought home to the conscience, Satan leads men to justify them-selves and to seek the sympathy of others in their course of sin.[5]

In writing to the Ephesians, the apostle Paul describes the Christian warfare as one "against the rulers of the darkness of this age, against spiri-tual hosts of wickedness in the heavenly places" (Ephesians 6:12). Earlier the apostle speaks of darkness from which Christians were brought out to "walk as children of light" and "have no fellowship with the unfruitful works of darkness" (Ephesians 5:8-11). Plainly said, the works of dark-ness are the works of sin—works committed in violation of God's law. The author of such works is the prince of evil, and to participate in such works is to come under the banner of Satan.

What is the condition of such who choose to follow the prince of darkness?

> Those who have chosen Satan as their leader and have been controlled by his power are not prepared to enter the presence of God. Pride, deception, licentiousness, cruelty, have become fixed in their characters. Can they enter heaven to dwell forever with those whom they despised and hated on earth? Truth will never be agreeable to a liar; meekness will not satisfy self-esteem and pride; purity is not acceptable to the corrupt; disinterested love does not appear attractive to the selfish.[6]

Such is the condition of the children of darkness. They have lost the sense of right and wrong, and cannot distinguish the difference between truth and error, light and darkness. And hence the apostle's warning to the Christian: "For what do righteousness and wickedness have in common? Or what fellowship can light have with darkness?" (2 Corinthians 6:14, NIV).

God of truth vs. father of lies

Christ spoke of Himself " 'I am the way, the truth, and the life. No one comes to the Father except through Me. If you had known Me, you would have known My Father also; and from now on you know Him and have seen Him' " (John 14:6, 7).

This is a profound statement of great significance in the history of the great controversy. While Satan was attacking the character of God as Creator of life, as Source of all truth, and as One who is love, Christ throws the challenge to the universe: to see Him for what He is and what He has come to reveal about His relationship with the Father. Christ came not only to reveal the truth about God, Satan, sin, and redemption; He is the Truth. Because He is the Incarnation of Truth in all its absoluteness, He is the only way to the Father. He claims an exclusivity that was under attack from Satan since his days in heaven. That exclusivity rested on the divinity of Christ. He, being One with the Father in character, nature, and purpose, now claims exclusivity as the only absolute manifestation of truth and the way to the Father. No one can claim to be the Redeemer, except Christ. No one can come to the Father, except through Christ.

Many have speculated what constitutes truth. Satan, working through human genius and intellect, has provided many answers through the course of history and he would delight in all of them. Some have defined truth as the first principle, from which all principles flow. Some have equated truth with a proposition that can be proven logically, such as the equation A=B, B=C, and therefore A=C. Others have seen truth in moral good or rational preciseness. Some would even define truth as loving and unselfish actions.

All these definitions of truth may be partially right, and it is in such partial rightness that Satan delights. Absolute truth is an anathema to Satan, for fullness of truth demands a clear definition between the Creator and the creature, between love and selfishness, between moral law and moralistic conduct, between faith in a personal God and belief in a supreme ideal. In short, absolute truth resides in the person of God, and that's what Satan hates. What's more, Satan knows to his horror that Ultimate Truth has put on human garb in Christ. The highway to God is wide open through the person of Jesus, and the doors of the kingdom are open to those who would walk that way in faith.

If Christ is the Truth that opened the doors of salvation, Satan is the " 'father of lies' " (John 8:44, NIV) who rejoices in leading humanity to join his rebellion against God. "From the beginning Satan has portrayed to men the gains to be won by transgression. Thus he seduced angels. Thus he tempted Adam and Eve to sin. And thus he is still leading multitudes away from obedience to God. The path of transgression is made to appear desirable; 'but the end thereof are the ways of death.' Proverbs 14:12."[7]

In addition to the falsehood Satan spread in heaven against God's character and His law, what other notable lies has he told? God told Adam and Eve that they would die if they ate the forbidden fruit, but Satan assured them that there was no such thing as death. Instead they would be immortal, and be like God (Genesis 3:4-5). That first lie has laid the foundation for an entire system of philosophy and religion that has stood in the way of God's truth and His redemptive purposes. The doctrine of the natural immortality of the soul undercuts the need of the Cross as a means of forgiveness, and thus attacks the very mission of Jesus. When the soul is immortal, with countless possibilities of existence, what need is there for salvation? What meaning is there to the biblical statement, "the wages of sin is death" (Romans 6:23)?

In our own time, Satan has not failed in his mission of propagating lies as truths. The doctrine of evolution, the denial of a personal God and the role of Christ as the Redeemer, the rejection of the authority of the Bible, the institution of a false Sabbath, spiritualism and the overwhelming attraction of the New Age mindsets, and many more doctrines are his lies that have no foundation in the Scriptures.

As the great controversy moves to its climax, more and more the test for God's people will be, What shall we do with Christ who is the Truth?

The Shepherd vs. the wolf

The final contrast we will examine between the contenders in the great controversy has to do with the relationship that Christ and Satan have with people. It is in that relationship and how we relate to that relationship that the great controversy is won or lost in individual lives. Christ described this relationship in these tender words:

> "I am the good shepherd. The good shepherd gives His life for the sheep. But a hireling, he who is not the shepherd, one who does not own the sheep, sees the wolf coming and leaves the sheep and flees; and the wolf catches the sheep and scatters them. The hireling flees because he is a hireling and does not care about the sheep. I am the good shepherd; and I know My sheep, and am known by My own" (John 10:11-14).

Consider the clear and sharp contrasts between Christ and Satan as to how they relate to people. Christ calls Himself the good Shepherd who cares for and nurtures the sheep. He is faithful to His mission of caring and nurturing the sheep, not as though He is paid to do, but as the One charged by His Father to look after the flock. Christ's faithfulness is so intimate that He knows the sheep by name. He calls them when they wander away. He waits for them when they loiter. He searches for them when they are lost. All of these indicate that Christ's knowledge and care of us as His flock are born out of an eternal faithfulness—a faithfulness that goes back to eternity when He pledged Himself as a surety to redeem the lost sinners.

As the good Shepherd,

> Jesus knows us individually, and is touched with the feeling of our infirmities. He knows us all by name. He knows the very house in which we live, the name of each occupant. He has at times given directions to His servants to go to a certain street in a certain city, to such a house, to find one of His sheep.
>
> Every soul is as fully known to Jesus as if he were the only one for whom the Saviour died. The distress of every one touches His heart. The cry for aid reaches His ear.[8]

Contrast this picture of the good Shepherd with that of the wolf. Satan is described as the wolf. He is out on the prowl to catch the sheep unawares. Some of these sheep refuse to come under the nurture of the good Shepherd and place themselves under the care of hirelings, agencies that are tutored and trained by Satan to pretend as shepherds. The hirelings have no real sacrificial commitment—no cross, so to speak—to protect and care for the lives of the sheep. Their work is one of pretension, and how many sheep have gone astray to be under the hirelings. But they eventually become the prey of the great and cunning wolf, Satan. Christ, the good Shepherd, died in order that we might live; but Satan, the wolf, lives in order that we may perish eternally. The wolf uses and manipulates the sheep away from the real Shepherd. The sheep that follow Christ know Him, obey Him, love Him, and will be saved and protected by Him. But the sheep who wander away or who choose to be under the loose and nominal care of the hireling make themselves objects of the attacks of the wolf.

Between the flock and the peril stands the good Shepherd. In view of the perilous dangers the wolf poses, should we not make the song of David our own: "The Lord is my Shepherd; I shall not want." There alone lies our safety in the great controversy.

---

1. *Patriarchs and Prophets*, p. 63.
2. *The Desire of Ages*, p. 19.
3. C. S. Lewis, *Christian Reflections*, ed. Walter Hooper (Glasgow: Collins, 1981), p. 52.
4. *Testimonies*, 4:207.
5. *The Great Controversy*, p. 500.
6. *Ibid.*, p. 542.
7. *Patriarchs and Prophets*, p. 720.
8. *The Desire of Ages*, pp. 479, 480.

CHAPTER

The War
Comes to Earth

When Satan was cast out of heaven, he shifted his theater of operation to this earth.

No longer free to stir up rebellion in heaven, Satan's enmity against God found a new field in plotting the ruin of the human race. In the happiness and peace of the holy pair in Eden he beheld a vision of the bliss that to him was forever lost. Moved by envy, he determined to incite them to disobedience, and bring upon them the guilt and penalty of sin. He would change their love to distrust and their songs of praise to reproaches against their Maker. Thus he would not only plunge these innocent beings into the same misery which he was himself enduring, but would cast dishonor upon God, and cause grief in heaven.[1]

Life anywhere is subject to law, and the newly created life on earth was no exception. When Adam and Eve were placed in the perfect surroundings of Eden, their life and function were subject to God's law. God clearly told them that their life and their dominion on earth were dependent on obedience to His will. Upon their choice, their failure to trust Him and obey His will plunged this earth into the cosmic conflict that Satan began in heaven and now has vowed to carry out on earth.

Adam and Eve: whose shall we be?

Perfection marked the creation of Adam and Eve. Genesis 1 records that each day's creation was "good." But when God concluded His creative work by placing the first human beings on earth, He looked upon His entire creation and pronounced that they were "very good" (Genesis 1:31). Moreover, there was something unique about the creation of our first parents. The Bible says that they were made "in the image of God" (Genesis 1:26, 27). This description is not used with regard to the creation of any other creature. In bestowing upon human beings "the image of God," the Creator has placed them in a unique place and position. God has chosen to share with them a part of His own character. That gives them freedom and creativity, dignity and worth, dominion and power over other creatures, self-consciousness and individuality. But Adam and Eve were not independent in the sense that they can live apart from God. As creatures, they were dependent on God, and responsible to Him. So they were called upon to exercise faith and trust in Him, worship Him and Him alone, and obey Him.

To make Adam and Eve understand this dependency in the God-human relationship, the Creator required them to obey His laws. Their lives depended upon this test of obedience and upon their understanding of God's supremacy. And so "God commanded the man, saying, 'Of every tree of the garden you may freely eat; but of the tree of the knowledge of good and evil you shall not eat, for in the day that you eat of it you shall surely die' " (Genesis 2:16, 17).

God laid out the choice before Adam and Eve without any ambiguity: trust, obey and live or distrust, disobey and die. In laying out the choice, God also warned that since they were created free, there is the possibility of yielding to disobedience. It was not as though Adam and Eve were ignorant of the cosmic conflict and the impending tempter out to deceive them.

Our first parents were not left without a warning of the danger that threatened them. Heavenly messengers opened to them the history of Satan's fall and his plots for their destruction, unfolding more fully the nature of the divine government, which the prince of evil was trying to overthrow.[2]

Yet at the approach of the tempter, Adam and Eve were not prepared to resist. The temptation does not lie in the tree of the knowledge of good and evil. There was nothing wrong with the fruit of the tree. But it was a test of the moral fiber and spiritual loyalty of our first parents. What kind of a choice would they make? Would they choose their Creator or the tempter? Would they trust His Word or heed to the false promise of Satan that they would not die as a result of eating the fruit but would be like God? Would they accept a life of trust and love and obedience to the Creator or would they opt for the tempter's offer of freedom, selfishness, and rebellion?

The sin of Adam and Eve is in trying to be equal to God. An impossibility for sure, but that's the temptation Satan placed before them: " 'For God knows that in the day you eat of it your eyes will be opened, and you will be like God, knowing good and evil' " (Genesis 3:5). The one who said in heaven, "I will be like the Most High," coveting the position of equality with God, and thus causing the war in heaven, now introduces the war on earth by placing before Adam and Eve a similar appeal. "Be like God, eat the fruit."

Satan's appeal was preceded by a lie. Against God's word that the eating of the fruit would lead to death, the tempter promised, " 'You will not surely die' " (Genesis 3:4). Adam and Eve chose to distrust God's word and heeded Satan. Their first allegiance was not to God, but to self and self's desire to be its own god.

Adam and Eve ate the forbidden fruit, but in that one act of disobedience plunged this earth and their own lives in sorrow and grief. The great controversy took roots on this earth. From then on human history has become a theater of contention between God and Satan, God still pleading, through His Spirit and His Son, through His Word and His covenants, for the fallen race to return to the family, and Satan using every manipulation to deceive humankind.

Some may ask, after seeing the result of free choice in the life of Lucifer, why did not God create beings who would be totally obedient? Such a question not only challenges the sovereignty of God but also His very character of love that can expect obedience only in an atmosphere of freedom and choice.

Without freedom of choice, his obedience would not have been voluntary, but forced. There could have been no development of character. Such a course would have been contrary to God's plan in dealing with the inhabitants of other worlds. It would have been unworthy of man as an intelligent being, and would have sustained Satan's charge of God's arbitrary rule.[3]

For a moment Satan delighted that he had triumphed—those whom God created "very good" could not keep even a simple requirement of God. But in the midst of human disobedience, God's love stepped forward, and the Creator unveiled His eternal plan to deal with sin and Satan and to save the fallen race. The Cross would prove forever to the universe that God is love, and His law is just and unchangeable.

The act of Christ in dying for the salvation of man would not only make heaven accessible to men, but before all the universe it would justify God and His Son in their dealing with the rebellion of Satan. It would establish the perpetuity of the law of God and would reveal the nature and the results of sin.[4]

Cain and Abel: whom shall we worship?

If Adam and Eve show the importance of unreserved obedience to God in the great controversy, the story of Cain and Abel illustrates the significance of worship in humanity's engagement in the cosmic conflict. Both Abel and Cain recognized the importance of worship, but the issue is, what kind of worship? Whom shall we worship? Does worship recognize the sovereignty of God and acknowledge His supremacy in all things? Do we come to worship God, fall at His feet, confess our sinfulness, and plead for His grace and forgiveness?

True worship has no room of self-adoration. It expects that we strip all pretensions to holiness or righteousness and come to the throne room of God and acknowledge our need for God's grace. Any act that glorifies self cannot be true worship, for in that very act is the seed of rebellion against, and a denial of, God's absolute prerogative of all creatures.

Both Cain and Abel knew what was involved in true worship. The clothing of Adam and Eve—the coats of a slain lamb's skin—symbolized the cost of sin and the way of redemption. "Without the shedding of blood there is no forgiveness" (Hebrews 9:22, NIV) was a lesson Adam and Eve learned and passed on as part of the worship of God. The lamb slain in Eden was a symbol of Christ—the Lamb of God—who would be slain on the cross for the sins of the world. To acknowledge the need for Christ and His shed blood is an important part of worship.

And here lies the failure of Cain. Fruits may be good. Vegetables are great. But that's not God's way of acknowledging Him as our Redeemer. Abel understood this and obeyed God's requirement and brought a lamb. But Cain, like Satan, chose to defy God's requirement and set about his own way of worship.

> Abel grasped the great principles of redemption. He saw himself a sinner, and he saw sin and its penalty, death, standing between his soul and communion with God. He brought the slain victim, the sacrificed life, thus acknowledging the claims of the law that had been transgressed. Through the shed blood he looked to the future sacrifice, Christ dying on the cross of Calvary; and trusting in the atonement that was there to be made, he had the witness that he was righteous, and his offering accepted.
>
> Cain had the same opportunity of learning and accepting these truths as had Abel. He was not the victim of an arbitrary purpose.... Abel chose faith and obedience; Cain, unbelief and rebellion.[5]

By his own choice to defy God's way of worship, Cain brought judgment upon himself. God rejected his worship. But rebellion does not end in one act; it adds act upon act, and makes one's heart hard and one's mind even more defiant against God and His requirements. That's the way Satan works. Cain's first sin led him to the second, and he murdered his own brother. Failure in worship leads to failure in fellowship. Those who cannot revere God can seldom care for what true human fellowship demands.

The defiant nature of Cain's act consists in that he would have his own way, and who was God to call him to account? Who was God to judge the merits of his worship? And why should he be his brother's keeper?

Cain could not stand Abel's love for God and righteousness toward

Him, and so did not hesitate to become the first murder—just as Satan did not consider the cost of becoming the first sinner. Cain had love for neither God nor his brother. Where there is no love, sin thrives, and Satan rejoices. Satan must have reveled at the sight of the first murder, for part of his scheme in the great controversy is to split humanity into irreconcilable fragments: man against woman, tribe against tribe, caste against caste, white against black, and so on. The more the divisions the more Satan delights at the possibility that he can win his case in the great controversy.

But through Christ, God has made it possible for these walls of partition to come tumbling down. "There is neither Jew nor Greek, there is neither slave nor free, there is neither male nor female; for you are all one in Christ Jesus" (Galatians 3:28). While it is Satan's purpose to create divisions within human fellowship, particularly the faith community, it is God's priority that through the death of Christ all may become members of one great family. Unity of Christian fellowship is a sure indication that we are on the Lord's side (John 17:21) in the great controversy, and that the gates of hell shall not prevail against us.

Noah and the Flood: rebellion and judgment

By the time biblical history comes down to the time of Noah, the great controversy witnessed both the righteous and the wicked populating the earth. But at the time of Noah, Satan was able to gain so much ground in his attempts to deceive humanity that the Bible records one of the saddest and most hopeful statements: "The Lord was grieved that he had made man on the earth, and his heart was filled with pain.... But Noah found favor [grace, KJV] in the eyes of the Lord" (Genesis 6:6-8, NIV). Sadness is found in the widespread presence of wickedness. Hope is seen that even in the cesspool of sin, there was Noah who found in God's grace the courage to live a righteous life. This shows that even as the great controversy rages around us, even as the wicked seem to be ever growing and sin becomes an accepted way, God's grace can make it possible for us to live righteously in accordance with His will.

Why was God's heart filled with pain? Genesis 6 tells us that God saw how great and perverse was the wickedness of humanity! In action and thought, humanity had become slave to the workings of Satan, and the time had come for God to pour out His judgment against such wickedness. Both the presence of widespread sin and the impending judgment caused God pain. Even though men of righteousness, such as Methuselah and Noah, lived, pleaded, and preached God's way of holiness, moral evil and spiritual wickedness had enveloped the earth.

As a result, God's judgment came upon Noah's generation in the form of a worldwide flood.

> Had the antediluvians believed the warning, and repented of their evil deeds, the Lord would have turned aside His wrath, as He afterward did from Nineveh. But by their obstinate resistance to the reproofs of conscience and the warnings of God's prophet, that generation filled up the measure of their iniquity, and became ripe for destruction.[6]

The Deluge was real. It accomplished a complete destruction of the world, except for those that believed in God and entered the ark of grace. Satan must have opposed Noah's preaching of righteousness and prediction of a worldwide deluge by saying that there could be no such catastrophe. That is always his way—to cast doubt on God's word. Even today he leads scholars of thought and science to question that there ever was a worldwide deluge, just to disbelieve the authority of God's Word. Likewise, he leads men and women to doubt that this world of sin is heading for its eventual annihilation with God's judgment by fire.

While the waters destroyed the world, God's grace was at work in that He saved Noah and his family. There lies the hope for those believe in the ultimate saving power of God. As part of his contention in the great controversy, Satan may mislead many to join him and reject the need for allegiance to God. But God's grace pursues the sinner as far and as long as the sinner would allow. God's love is limitless, and His justice certain. As a symbol of that love and at the conclusion of His judgment, God made a covenant with Noah (Genesis 9:8-17). God's mercy looked down upon the human race and made a pledge that never again would the earth be destroyed by a flood. As a sign of His assurance, God set up a rainbow in the sky.

The New Testament often compares Noah's time to the end time in which we live. " 'As the days of Noah were,' " Jesus warned, " 'so also will the coming of the Son of Man be' " (Matthew 24:37). The warning of Jesus is to be taken seriously. As it was in the days of Noah, so it will also be in the end time: sin will abound, wickedness will reign, God's claims will be questioned, His Word will be doubted, His message of the ultimate judgment destroying this world of sin will be rejected. But suddenly and surely, God's final judgment will come (2 Peter 3:5-7). Only those who place their trust in God and His grace will find salvation and refuge. Only they will taste the sweetness of the victory in the great controversy.

The Tower of Babel: trust in human strength

The spirit of distrust in God and trust in one's own strength, instilled in our foreparents by Satan, never leaves the human heart. Both saints and sinners are continually tempted to trust in self. "I am the captain of my soul and the master of my fate," has become the rallying cry of humans ever since Adam and Eve crossed the frontiers of holiness. Part of the Christian warfare is to resist self's perpetual desire to become one's own god. Hence Paul's call to crucify self in order that we might live for God (Galatians 2:20).

The folly of trusting in one's own strength is well illustrated by the building of the Tower of Babel. The generation that built that tower issued a call for their collective strength to be pooled together as a protection against another flood. " 'Come, let us build ourselves a city, and a tower whose top is in the heavens; let us make a name for ourselves, lest we be scattered abroad over the face of the whole earth' " (Genesis 11:4).

There is nothing wrong in building a city, nothing wrong in being artistic or creative. But when that act of human intelligence is to boost one's self-pride or to mock at God's Word and promises, beware! Babylon is not far away. Note several factors that underlie the building of the Tower of Babel.

First, it is a distrust of God's Word and covenant. God had assured that " 'never again shall there be a flood to destroy the earth' " (Genesis 9:11). But the people did not believe in divine assurance. They, under the guidance of Satan, doubted God's Word. They sought protection in themselves from any possible worldwide catastrophe. Is this not one aspect of the great controversy: salvation in self-righteousness rather than in Christ's promise and covenant?

Second, it is a trust in their own selves. "Let us build ourselves a city," they said. In that city that will reach to the skies, they sought their protection and safety. Trust in self as opposed to trust in God is at the root cause of every evil and sin. Satan's origin was in self-trust and self-exaltation. The people of Babel sought to establish a government for themselves, not controlled by God's covenant, but regulated by their own self-will.

Their confederacy was founded in rebellion; a kingdom established for self-exaltation, but in which God was to have no rule or honor. Had this confederacy been permitted, a mighty power would have borne sway to banish righteousness—and with it peace, happiness, and security—from the earth. For the divine statutes, which are "holy and just and good" (Romans 7:12), men were endeavoring to substitute laws to suit the purpose of their own selfish and cruel hearts.[7]

Third, it is an act of willful disobedience to God's purposes. God's command at creation was that humanity should populate the entire earth (Genesis 1:28). After the Flood, there was no change in that purpose, but the children of Babel sought to renounce God's purposes and establish a community that would be a symbol of their own strength. They sought power and glory in self-deification.

The result was God's intervention. His purpose to populate the earth was fulfilled as a result of the confusion in language. Satan stood defeated.

The schemes of the Babel builders ended in shame and defeat. The monument to their pride became the memorial of their folly. Yet men are continually pursuing the same course—depending upon self, and rejecting God's law. It is the principle that Satan tried to carry out in heaven; the same that governed Cain in presenting his offering.[8]

---

1. *Patriarchs and Prophets,* p. 52.
2. *Ibid.,* p. 52.
3. *Ibid.,* p. 49.
4. *Ibid.,* p. 69.
5. *Ibid.,* p. 72.
6. *Ibid.,* p. 97.
7. *Ibid.,* p. 123.
8. *Ibid.*

CHAPTER 5

Winning and Losing

To a large extent, the Bible is the history of the great controversy between Christ and Satan as it is fought on our earth—the lesson book of the universe. And the history is told in the lives of men and women who had to choose between God and Satan. Some were winners. Some were losers. Even as God's Spirit continually attempts to reveal the power and purpose of His grace to redeem sinners, Satan makes each human being a target of his allurement or attack. Every person, especially those that claim to be God's servants, comes under the beguiling efforts of Satan to shift their loyalty, to deny their Creator, and to view God's law as unnecessary. During such struggles, the battle cry of the great controversy is simple but pointed: Whom will you serve?

The Bible speaks of real people who faced this challenge and struggled with the need to obey God. Their winning and losing depended upon the choices that they made. While Satan's position is that God's law is arbitrary, harsh, and impossible to keep, God's dealing with His people shows that a life of obedience is possible when that life is placed under God's power and grace. Surrender to God is the key for a life of spiritual victory. For the God who commands is also the One who enables.

We shall now review some of the great characters of the Bible—how they won and how they lost, and what we can learn from them even as we fight our battles in the great controversy.

46

Joseph: sin as an offence against God

Joseph! Favorite of his father's twelve children. Recipient of special gifts from the one who should have loved all of his children alike. Dreamer of visions of what God had in store for him. Target of jealousy of his brothers. Protected and guarded by an overaffectionate father, his life did not quite begin until he faced the reality of choices. The query of the great controversy, "Whom will you serve?" faced Joseph squarely in the face in the form of a beautiful, young, and seductive woman.

Joseph's confrontation took place in Egypt's high places—in the palace of Potiphar, the captain of Pharaoh's official guards. Such high places and such heathen countries—then as now—paid little attention to morality or godliness, and it is easy for Satan under such circumstances to divert attention of men and women from the demands of God's moral law, and indeed make a mockery of what sin is all about. Against that context we must view the moral victory of Joseph over the daily assaults of the tempter in the form of a seductive woman.

"Well-built and handsome" (Genesis 39:6, NIV), Joseph stood at the threshold of a choice that would decide on whose side he was. Temptation opened its doors wide and invited him to have the pleasures of sensuality in the form of a young and equally beautiful woman. Consider the pressures of this temptation. Here was the bed of the forbidden zone without the fear of being caught. Here was romance and sexual passion in a palace where the two were alone. Here was a society that tolerated sexual immorality. Here was the possibility of climbing high in the professional ladder of Egypt. Above all, here were the whispers of the great tempter that crossing the sexual frontier was no great matter: after all, everybody does it.

Potiphar's wife pursued him "day by day " (Genesis 39:10). Sin never gives up. The forbidden fruit always seems sweet, and grows sweeter by the day. Sensual looks, conniving words, Egypt's best perfume, and above all a lion seeking its prey were all put to work. But to no avail. Joseph's answer was clear: " 'How then can I do this great wickedness, and sin against God?' " (Genesis 39:9).

A traveling salesman confessed to his pastor one day that he had gotten himself into an illicit affair. "I couldn't help it," he said. "You don't understand the outside pressures and stresses I was in." The pastor responded: "Couldn't help it? Outside pressures? Whatever happened to your inside braces?"

Joseph had his inside braces intact. His God was the Source of his strength. To him, the issue was not illicit. To him, it was not crossing the forbidden zone of human sexuality. To him, it was a choice between God and Satan. The evil one presented to Joseph another forbidden fruit in the form of a seductive and willing woman. But Joseph "refused" (Genesis 39:8) to cross the line of His commitment to God. His choice was a costly one and landed him in jail. True discipleship to God is always costly, but it is better to be on the Lord's side than on the enemy's.

What were those inner braces that stood by Joseph in the time of his worst trial? An unreserved commitment to God. A sense of right and wrong. A spiritual maturity that defines illicit sex as sin against God. A moral integrity that cannot be bought or sold. A transformed soul that leads one to resist the devil and flee from evil.

Joseph was a good man. But before he was good, he was godly. Character, after all, is what a person is in the dark. Treachery may put a person in prison. The devil may crush the spirit of one who remains loyal to God. But in the end, the Sun of Righteousness does shine upon those loyal to Him. "The Lord was with Joseph and showed Him mercy" (Genesis 39:21). Joseph's "whole future life depended upon the decision of the moment. Would principle triumph? Would Joseph still be true to God? With inexpressible anxiety, angels looked upon the scene."[1]

What if Joseph had sinned and later repented and turned to God for forgiveness? Would God have forgiven him? Yes, He would have. But the character of Joseph would not have remained a bright star in the firmament of the moral sky—an object lesson for everyone tempted to stand firm and resist, a source of joy and satisfaction to God and angels who were looking down into Potiphar's palace with "inexpressible anxiety."

Charles Swindoll writes: "The truth evidenced in Joseph's life is for all of us—unmarried, divorced, remarried, man or woman, young or old. Whatever your situation, no matter how alluring or pleasurable or momentarily delightful the bait looks, don't linger. Claim Christ, and operating under the control of His power, stand strong in His might. Right now, this very moment, determine to be a Joseph. Make up your mind to join his ranks—and from this day forward, resist."[2]

Moses: eyes on the Promised Land

In the history of the great controversy, Moses played a significant role—not against one individual, but against a range of forces—forging a nation out of battered tribes, who had nearly lost their identity in slavery. Moses kept his eyes focused on the promises of God, and by faith chose "to suffer affliction with the people of God than to enjoy the passing pleasures of sin, esteeming the reproach of Christ greater riches than the treasures in Egypt" (Hebrews 11:25-26).

Moses' choice was clear. He will serve His God no matter what the cost, and he would preserve a nation that God would use to bring the Messiah and usher in the message of salvation to all the world. But Satan hoped to win the great controversy and prevent this from happening.

However, the patience of Moses and his unfailing trust in God's guidance enabled him to lead a people to the borders of the Promised Land. He became God's man in history. As such, he set an example in the kind of choices one must make in life.

Consider his refusal to be called the son of Pharaoh's daughter (Hebrews 11:24). This was no easy choice. Egypt's throne was his to assume, and as Pharaoh, Moses would have climbed the heights of glory. Satan welcomed such a choice and saw in that a seeming victory for his cause. But the man of God was made of sterner stuff. Educated in all the wisdom and philosophy of Egypt, trained in all the military skills of a great army, skilled in the intricacies of administration, Moses chose to use his education, his skills, and his training not to serve an earthly throne but to serve the God of heaven.

Consider his choice "to suffer affliction with the people of God." Those people were not easy ones to lead. Egyptian bondage not only destroyed their dignity and self-worth, but deprived them of a true understanding of their role and destiny in history. They were a people who were in affliction—not just physical, but also intellectual, emotional, and above all, spiritual. What was Moses to do with such deprived people? But Moses knew that his responsibility was to obey God's call to lead "the people of God." When God revealed Himself in the burning bush and told Moses, " 'I have seen the affliction of my people who are in Egypt' " (Exodus 3:7, RSV), Moses saw the people in a new light. They were not simply slaves; they were not simply a people without any identity; they were not even people of Moses. They were God's, and God would complete the job of liberating them. And so Moses cast his lot with His people. The choice was another blow to Satan's scheme to deny Israel a role in the coming of the Messiah.

Think of Moses the preserver of God's Word, His law, and His worship. In addition to liberating God's people, Moses faithfully recorded God's Word. Were it not for Moses, we would not have the narrative of Creation and the story of God's redemptive role from Adam to Israel's approach to the Promised Land. Were it not for him, we would not have had the written moral law of God. The first five books of the Bible, the sanctuary system, and all the revelation of the character of God that we know from them—we owe these to the commitment of Moses.

But Satan worked hard to distract Moses. One specific sin (Numbers 20:7-11) caused God to keep Moses out of the Promised Land, and Satan hoped surely this extreme penalty imposed on so great a leader would leave him so depressed that he might eventually deny his faith in God. But Moses' allegiance to God was not based on what he would get; it was total, and it was unconditional. As a result, God "did not forget or forsake His servant. The God of heaven understood the suffering that Moses had endured; He had noted every act of faithful service through those long years of conflict and trial. On the top of Pisgah, God called Moses to an inheritance infinitely more glorious than the earthly Canaan."[3] He resurrected Moses and took him to His presence (Matthew 17:1-3; Jude 9).

Samson: missed opportunities

Samson was a miracle child. His birth was the direct result of a divine promise for a divine purpose. His mission was to free Israel from the oppression of the Philistines, and to this task he was dedicated even before he was born. Samson's parents were charged with this mission to train him up in order that he may fulfill his role in God's plan. As a sign of this divine setting apart, he was to be a Nazirite. Taking the Nazirite vow signified continued consecration to a specific God-ordained purpose, and in the case of Samson, this purpose was to bring about the deliverance of Israel. A noble purpose. And the vow was just as noble and significant, and involved that the person should not eat of any product of the wine, should not approach a dead body, and should not let a razor come upon his hair.

His role in the great controversy was to assure Israel their freedom and to be a judge over God's people. He thus had an opportunity to be a moral and spiritual leader, keeping Israel on the high ground of God's calling, and maintain the sanctity of God's special leadership among His people. But Samson's life is an illustration of missed opportunities by making wrong choices.

First, there was the marriage to a Philistine girl. A man called to deliver the people of God from the Philistine oppression chooses a Philistine girl, for no reason except " 'she pleases me well' " (Judges 14:3). Against the pleading of his parents, against the long-range mission that was his, Samson chose to please self. By putting self on the top of his priorities, he placed himself in a complex situation that led to shame. And the marriage was a failure. Although Samson took revenge and made the Philistine home pay a heavy price in terms of lives and property lost, was this a part of his mission?

Second, there was the missed opportunity of having constant faith. Samson's life oscillated between confidence and doubt, between choosing God's way and compromising with the devil. Whenever he yielded himself to the Spirit of God, the Spirit came mightily upon him (Judges 14:19; 15:14) and he could shatter the enemies of God's people. But in small matters like thirst, he could not trust God that he could provide him with water. " 'Shall I die of thirst?' " he asked the Creator (Judges 15:18). Where was his faith? The God who delivered him many times from the Philistines and led him in the battle against God's enemies—shall He not care for his needs? A vacillating faith is a weak faith, and Satan takes advantage of that. In this case of Samson, this state of unsteadiness finally led him to be captured by the Philistines.

Third, there was the missed opportunity of being a leader. Although Samson judged Israel for twenty years, he did not seize the opportunity to unite Israel under God's leadership. Although the children of Israel rejoiced whenever Samson crushed their enemies, they never fully united behind him. Perhaps he did not do enough to persuade Israel that what He did was a result of God's will, and not his strength. If he had, the history of Israel at that time would have been different. A failure to recognize God's leadership, in spite of what success one may have, leads eventually for Satan to take the upper hand.

Fourth, there was the missed opportunity of recognizing one's sin and returning to God. Samson's first marriage led to a disaster. That should have been enough to teach him the need to obey God. But Satan does not give up so easily, and his persistent quest for Samson's destruction came in the form of another woman. Samson fell to the bewitching sensuality of Delilah, and in eagerness to fulfill his selfish passions, he broke the vow to which he was born. First came the wine. Then came the razor. The pleasure of Delilah became more important than the privilege of duty to God. Whenever self takes priority over God, we are on dangerous ground. Samson's strength finally gave way, and he reached the gutters of humiliation and capture.

However, God did fulfill his promise of deliverance from the Philistines in answer to the final prayer of Samson, but Samson died with the Philistines (Judges 16:25-31).

Had Samson been true to his divine calling, the purpose of God could have been accomplished in his honor and exaltation. But he yielded to temptation and proved untrue to his trust, and his mission was fulfilled in defeat, bondage, and death. Physically, Samson was the strongest man upon the earth; but in self-control, integrity, and firmness, he was one of the weakest of men. Many mistake strong passions for a strong character, but the truth is that he who is mastered by his passions is a weak man. The real greatness of the man is measured by the power of the feelings that he controls, not by those that control him.[4]

Self-indulgence is Satan's great ally in the great controversy!

David: down, but not out

Chosen as a lad, David was called to play his role in the great controversy. And for the most part he did. He was the slayer of Goliath. He was the builder of a great kingdom. He established the city of Jerusalem. He restored the ark of the covenant. He was the sweet singer of Israel, and bequeathed to history under the inspiration of the Holy Spirit some of the finest songs in the world. His rulership and commitment to God were held as a standard by which all who succeeded him were measured. God Himself testified of him as " ' "a man after My own heart" ' " (Acts 13:22).

Yet, it is such men and women, who are loyal and devoted to God, that are the special target of Satan in the great controversy. The enemy is too cunning, and our flesh is too weak, and Satan chooses his own timing and method to attack the best of God's saints to prove his point that obedience to God's law is not possible. David's sin against Bathsheba (2 Samuel 11; 12) reveals that no saint is immune to the wiles of the devil.

Where did David go wrong? Once again the answer is to be located in the very nature of sin: it is in trusting self and rebelling against God.

> It was the spirit of self-confidence and self-exaltation that prepared the way for David's fall . . . instead of relying in humility upon the power of Jehovah, he began to trust to his own wisdom and might. As soon as Satan can separate the soul from God, the only Source of strength, he will seek to arouse the unholy desires of man's carnal nature. The work of the enemy is not abrupt; it is not, at the outset, sudden and startling; it is a secret undermining of the strongholds of principle.[5]

With great relish Satan must have looked at David's fall, adding the sin of adultery to the sin of murder. Even a "man after God's own heart" could not keep the law. Satan must have rejoiced at the victory he had won over God's chosen leader. But the rejoicing did not last long, for the promise of God always stands by His people: "If we confess our sins, He is faithful and just to forgive us our sins and to cleanse us from all unrighteousness" (1 John 1:9).

David's confession and repentance is recorded in Psalm 51. David acknowledged his sin as an act against God. "Against You, You only, have I sinned, and done this evil in Your sight" (Psalm 51:4). Sin in whatever shape or form it takes is always against God; it is a rupture in one's relationship with God. In Psalm 32:1, 2, David uses four important words to define sin:

> *transgression*—a deliberate, willful violation of God's norm;
> *sin*—an act that deviates from what God has marked out;
> *iniquity*—an act of crookedness and perverse behavior; and
> *deceit*—an attempt to cover up and evade obligation.

David confessed that he is guilty of all these, and he was aware of what sin had done to him: the wasting away of body, groaning with guilt, the inescapability of divine judgment, and the drying up of his soul's strength (Psalm 32:2-4). So diabolic is sin in its effects that there is nothing that the sinner can do to escape from its clutches (Romans 7:24).

But where sin abounds grace does much more abound (Romans 5:20). That is the Creator's provision for a fallen saint, and David grasped this immediately, confessed his sins, repented of them, and pleaded with God:

> Have mercy upon me, O God, according to Your lovingkindness; according to the multitude of Your tender mercies, blot out my transgressions. Wash me thoroughly from my iniquity, and cleanse me from my sin. For I acknowledge my transgressions, and my sin is always before me…. Create in me a clean heart, O God, and renew a steadfast spirit within me (Psalm 51:1-3, 10).

Where true confession and repentance is, God comes to the rescue of the sinning soul and forgives. He gives a clean heart that the repentant soul may remain steadfast. David obtained that clean heart, and remains to this day an example of the steadfastness of God to stand by His soldiers in the great controversy.

Elijah and Ahab: great controversy in contrast

The battle between good and evil, between God and Satan, between Elijah and Ahab, was joined on Mount Carmel. Between the prophet of God and King Ahab and the priests of Baal stood an altar that showed the true nature of the rebellion, and revealed that victory always belonged to God and those on His side. But a choice needed to be made, and that choice was spelt out by the prophetic word: " 'How long will you falter between two opinions? If the LORD is God, follow Him; but if Baal, follow him' " (1 Kings 18:21).

Elijah's challenge is timeless. It is addressed to those who wavered between God and Baal. To those who seek in the church a comfortable pew and a compromising message. To those who find in Christianity not the power of the gospel to convict and save but a tool that brings social status and approval. To those who hop between truth and error, moral uprightness and humanistic minimum, the perils of the Cross and the profits of the comfort zone.

The lone prophet was pitted against 450 priests of Baal. But one person with God is a majority. To such, the victory of Mount Carmel is sure and certain, just as it was to Elijah. His victory over Ahab and the priests of Baal was the victory of an unwavering faith in God.

Faith such as this is needed in the world today—faith that will lay hold on the promises of God's word and refuse to let go until Heaven hears. Faith such as this connects us closely with Heaven, and brings us strength for coping with the powers of darkness.[6]

1. *Patriarchs and Prophets,* p. 217.
2. Charles Swindoll, *Joseph* (Nashville: Word Publishing, 1998), p. 36.
3. *Patriarchs and Prophets,* p. 479.
4. *Ibid.,* pp. 567, 568.
5. *Ibid.,* pp. 717, 718.
6. *Prophets and Kings,* p. 157.

CHAPTER

Faith
Amid Turmoil

"Without faith it is impossible to please God, because any one who comes to him must believe that he exists and that he rewards those who earnestly seek him" (Hebrews 11:6, NIV). The relationship between humans and God is a faith-based relationship. We must believe that He exists. We must believe that He created us. We must believe that only in Him we can find our salvation. Without that basic faith, there can be no proper relationship with God.

Faith is trusting God—believing that He loves us and knows best what is for our good. Thus, instead of our own, it leads us to choose His way. In place of our ignorance, it accepts His wisdom; in place of our weakness, His strength; in place of our sinfulness, His righteousness. Our lives, ourselves, are already His; faith acknowledges His ownership and accepts its blessing.[1]

Satan knows the importance of faith in the Christian life. It is his studied purpose in the great controversy to shake the faith of God's people. The Bible is filled with the stories of men and women whose faith Satan attempted to weaken and destroy. His instruments are many and varied—physical affliction, sickness, betrayal, spiritual despondency, captivity, persecution, and even death—but his purpose remains constant: cripple our faith in God and His redeeming grace, and thus win us over to his side in the great controversy.

But genuine faith claims victory over Satan's onslaughts, for it is based not on human strength, but on the unfailing resources of God's grace. Job, Abraham, Esther and many more stand out as heroes who have won a decisive victory in the great cosmic conflict. Their victory lay not in what they have done, but what God's grace has done in their lives. They trusted in God, and God did not fail them.

> The Lord can work most effectually through those who are most sensible of their own insufficiency, and who will rely upon Him as their leader and source of strength. He will make them strong by uniting their weakness to His might, and wise by connecting their ignorance with His wisdom.[2]

Job: faith on trial

The primary lesson we learn from Job is not why the righteous suffer, but how the stability of faith can be maintained in the midst of suffering. How does one affirm faith in God in the face of suffering beyond endurance or explanation? How does one explain Auschwitz, the killing fields, ethnic cleansing, tribal vengeance, or slavery and still speak in the same breath of the love of God? How does one lose a joyful five-year-old to a drunken driver and say, "Though I walk through the valley of the shadow of death, I fear no evil" (Psalm 23:4, RSV)?

The life of Job is a cry in the midst of pain. It acknowledges that sunset and sunrise, dark clouds and bright skies, and tears of grief and smiles of fulfillment are not just the ebb and flow of life that we need to fatalistically accept and go on—but they are moments in life's journey in which faith and prayer need to shine on and confess, " 'I know that my Redeemer lives' " (Job 19:25).

How can such faith stability be maintained? Job offers a simple formula: Know your God and live in faith till the end. At the foundation of a stable faith life is a knowledge of God—not a theoretical knowledge, important as it may be, but a personal, relational, knowledge. Job knew His God in that intimate way, and inspiration describes his character in three beautiful phrases: he "was blameless and upright," he "feared God," and "shunned evil" (Job 1:1).

That he chose to live a life within the context of God and resisted every temptation to live otherwise—in spite of the fleeting fortunes of time and of the uncertainties of space—became for one critical moment a point of contention in the throne room of the Universe. Of course, God knew the implicit and trusting faith of Job. But it is such implicit faith that comes under the shattering blows of the father of disbelief and lies. Why would Satan be interested in attacking one of his own? Thus, the integrity of Job, the believer, becomes the focus of every adversity the adversary can mount.

" 'Does Job fear God for nothing?' " (Job 1:9) was Satan's challenge. He said,

> "I know men like Job. They follow God because He blesses them. Their faith in God means nothing when adversity hits. When pain and suffering come, their faith will turn to doubt and in their doubt they will deny God to His face."

But God knows His own—the unshakeable, the enduring, and the eternally committed ones to whom "to know God is life eternal" and nothing else matters. In a world whose temporary ruler is Satan, he has often successfully turned religion into a materialistic farce, faith into a commodity for sale to the highest bidder, and prayer into self-fulfillment of the Pharisee or the opium of the poor. But in such a world, "there was a man . . . whose name was Job." In the cosmic battle of the great controversy, Job was drawn in unawares—but not unready—and the eternal battle for the soul of this saint has left for us a historic lesson on the meaning of faith.

The lesson is simple: faith is not the preoccupation of the fleeting moment, but the persistent demand of the entire life. With his children dead, his wealth looted, his livestock destroyed, his wife urging him to renounce his faith in a God who is seemingly not there to help him, his life hanging on a thread, his friends questioning his integrity and faith, what was Job to live for? Human frailty showed up in Job's cursing the day he was born (3:1-3), his wishing that death would be a better choice than the bitterness of life (6:8-13), and his cry for vindication (16:6-17). And yet, the underlying strength of Job's faith was seen in his ability to praise God in the midst of emptiness (" 'The Lord gave, and the Lord has taken away; blessed be the name of the Lord' " [1:21]), and in his refusal to betray His name (2:10).

Note some reasons why Job's faith remained strong, even though his suffering seemed unbearable and undeserved. *First, faith at all costs.* Life or death, joy or pain, divine embrace or Satanic assault, Job cried out that his faith in God shall not be moved. " 'Though He slay me, yet will

I trust Him' " (Job 13:15). Faith placed in the person of God enables one to pray: "In the midst of no hope, I shall have hope."

Second, faith is costly but purposive. While Job's friends readily assigned blame for his predicament to his sin, Job refuted his friends. He did not have a good answer as to why the righteous suffer, but he knew that faith in God was not for sale. He admitted that faith is costly, and with a perspective so prominent in the New Testament, he affirmed: " 'When He has tested me, I shall come forth as gold' " (Job 23:10). The end result of a life of faith was a character as pure as gold, strong enough to withstand Satan in his assaults.

Third, faith is eschatological. True faith is rooted in Christian eschatology. "Thy kingdom come" becomes the rallying point for Christian faith. "If a man dies, shall he live again?" asked Job, and hastened to add that he would wait till that day of deliverance. "Weeping may endure for a night, but joy comes in the morning" (Psalm 30:5) is the way the psalmist expresses Christian hope. More than anyone else, Job knew this. The tortures of life may seem long and painful, but they fade away like the dew of the morning, when in faith and hope the believer looks at everything from the perspective of what God has prepared. Eschatology opens wide the door of endurance: " 'I know that my Redeemer lives, and He shall stand at last on the earth' " (Job 19:25). That final day of earth's history will bring finality and closure to sin and pain.

Abraham: covenant faith

Covenant is a key theme of the Scriptures, and it plays a crucial role in the understanding of the great controversy. The word signifies the basis on which a relationship between two parties can be maintained and includes the responsibilities and privileges of both parties. It is an agreement, a contract. The Bible uses the word to signify an agreement not between two equal parties, but between the infinite God and finite human beings. It is an agreement in which God has taken the initiative to restore the relationship that was lost because of sin. The restored relationship is based on God's everlasting love, and the response of humans to trust God, love and obey Him. It is here that the covenant becomes crucial to the cosmic conflict: on the one hand, God is committed to fulfilling His promises, and on the other, Satan diabolically plots to make the human reject God's covenant relationship.

God's plan and Satan's plot are well illustrated in the covenant God made with Abraham. God revealed the essentials of this covenant when He called Abraham out of his native land with a promise:

"Get out of your country, from your family and from your father's house, to a land that I will show you. I will make you a great nation; I will bless you and make your name great; and you shall be a blessing. I will bless those who bless you, and I will curse him who curses you; and in you all the families of the earth shall be blessed" (Genesis 12:1-3).

When God repeated the covenant again (Genesis 15:1-5), Abraham became confounded, for thus far he had no children. How would God fulfill the promise? Through his faithful servant Eliezer? God said, No. The promise would be fulfilled through " 'one who will come from your own body,' " assured God (Genesis 15:1-5). God asked Abraham to look to the skies. As the stars are numberless so shall the family God will establish through Abraham be, and "he believed in the Lord, and He accounted it to him for righteousness" (Genesis 15:6).

Years rolled by. Still no children. And Satan put a novel suggestion in Abraham's mind. Abraham and Sarah planned to help out God. Through Hagar, Sarah's maid, Abraham obtained a son, but this child was not to be the means of fulfilling the covenant. In the redemptive promise of God, no human can have a share. God had His own plan and time, and humans have to wait upon Him and accept His way. Self does not initiate or fulfill the covenant promise; it only has to accept what God provides.

The covenant was repeated again (Genesis 17:1-11) and along with the covenant, God provided circumcision as a sign of the surety of the covenant. The sign of sealing the covenant was provided, but no heir in sight. Faith stood tested. Not until all hope seemed to have been lost, not until Abraham and Sarah were well past the age of childbearing, did God make His move. The faith child, Isaac, was born. But the faith and joy of Abraham were now tested in the most severe, un-Godlike way. God called upon Abraham to sacrifice Isaac.

What was God trying to do? Was this some sort of a divine-human drama? God promises. Then He delays. God gives the sign and again delays. God brings about the miracle of the promised child, and now demands that he be sacrificed? Is God playing games with Abraham? "Satan was near to whisper doubts and unbelief, but Abraham resisted his suggestions."[3] The child was God's. The child was born when Abraham and Sarah were dead to childbearing prospects. Would not the same God, concluded Abraham, be "able to raise him up, even from the dead" (Hebrews 11:19)?

Thus, in absolute faith, Abraham cast his lot on God's side. Faith in Him cannot be compromised, however great the whisper of the evil one may be. God gave Isaac. God asks for him. Abraham's only response was to obey. The covenant relationship was that simple. God's demand may seem illogical to the human mind, but we are to obey because God says so.

Abraham chose the altar of obedience against a thousand alternatives human schemes and devilish whispers could offer.

> Abraham's great act of faith stands like a pillar of light, illuminating the pathway of God's servants in all succeeding ages. Abraham did not seek to excuse himself from doing the will of God.... Abraham was human; his passions and attachments were like ours; ... [but] he did not stay to reason with his aching heart. He knew that God is just and righteous in all His requirements, and he obeyed the command to the very letter.[4]

The final outcome of the test stands for all ages as a testimony of the victory of genuine faith. Faith that leaps across human emotions and reasoning and embraces the promises of God is able to say, " 'God will provide' " (Genesis 22:8). The provision of God ultimately saved Isaac, confirmed faith, and affirmed that the covenant is His to be fulfilled. Our duty is only to obey Him that it fails not. In that faith and obedience lies our victory in the great controversy.

Esther: one can make a difference

The word "God" does not appear anywhere in the book of Esther. Yet through and through it is the story of the God who sees, hears, and acts. It is one of the finest illustrations of how God intervenes in history to protect His people and His purposes against the wily schemes of Satan. It also emphasizes how one person can make a difference for good in the movement of history.

One prophet, Elijah, stands alone and brings down the wicked house of Ahab and Jezebel. One John the Baptist confronts an entire nation and prepares the way for the Messiah. One Peter trumpets the meaning of the Cross on the Day of Pentecost and launches a movement that tears apart the kingdom of Satan and turns the world upside down for God.

One Paul takes on the world for God. One Luther changed the darkest hour in Christianity into a glorious dawn. One Carey carries the tools of a cobbler and the Word of God and opens the world of mission by setting off to India. One feeble little girl surrenders herself to God, and Ellen White becomes the messenger of a movement that has taken the global mission of Revelation 14 to the entire world.

One Esther, with prayer and poise, takes her stand for her God, and saves the entire chosen race from whom the Messiah would come. Arraigned against her was not just Haman and his tribe, but the hosts of Satan. Here was one of the most crucial battles in the great controversy. With one strike, Satan could crush the entire covenant community of God. He "was trying to rid the earth of those who preserved the knowledge of the true God."[5]

Two expressions in the book of Esther deserve special note: " 'For such a time as this,' " and " 'If I perish, I perish!' " (Esther 4:14-16).

First, in the great controversy in which we are engaged, when God calls, take a stand now. Time and tide waits for no man, says an old saying. And this is specially so when it comes to standing for God and His truth. In a history-making plea, Esther's uncle, Mordecai, sends the queen this appeal to take her stand against Haman's plot:

> "For if you remain completely silent at this time, relief and deliverance will arise for the Jews from another place, but you and your father's house will perish. Yet who knows whether you have come to the kingdom for such a time as this?" (Esther 4:14).

God works in time and history, and He will not let His purposes fail or His mission collapse. But He calls upon human instruments to do His will. If Esther had failed to do her duty at that critical time, she would have met her doom then and faced eternal judgment later. God's purpose would have been fulfilled through another means. But God's love is so great that He did not wish Esther to miss her opportunity of service to Him. He did not want her to work with Haman as an instrument of Satan. So He sent the gentle and forceful message through Mordecai: Stand now or lose forever. Being the queen provides no security against Satan's attack.

Second, in the great controversy, our life is not as important as God's plan. Those who do not learn this lesson have not learned at all what it means to be God's follower. Esther was God's follower. The danger to one's spiritual heritage, one's faith, and the attack of an enemy somehow bring out the best in a soul that is hinged to God. Suddenly, Esther was transformed from the winner of a beauty parade to being a humble handmaid of God; from the queen of Persia to a bearer of God's torch; from the sex symbol of Shushan to a servant of God's mission. And her determination was as firm as Mordecai's mission. "I will do it. If I perish, I perish." Death in standing for God's cause is to be preferred to the pleasure and ease of the palace. And because Esther took her stand, God's cause triumphed and Satan stood defeated.

Ellen White's commentary on Esther (*Prophets and Kings,* pp. 598–606) argues that the death proclaimed against the Jews is symbolic of "the decree that will finally go forth against the … true church" (p. 605). "The same spirit that in ages past led men to persecute the true church, will in the future lead to the pursuance of a similar course toward those who maintain their loyalty to God. Even now preparations are being made for this last great conflict" (ibid.). Mrs. White further identifies the battlefield as "the last great conflict in the controversy between truth and error" (p. 606), involving God's law and Sabbath. In that final conflict, the Lord will certainly vindicate His people, just as He did during Esther's time.

But we need to stand, like Esther did. In the great controversy there is no room for passivity. No place for just onlookers. God expects us to stand, speak, and if necessary, die. In the battle of the Lord, we have no option to ask: should we or should we not? Christian warfare is a call to arms, to fight the battle of faith, to stand by the Lord's side, to match our convictions with courage, and to fight the evil one. Isaac Watts's hymn says it well:

Am I a soldier of the cross,
A follower of the Lamb?
And shall I fear to own His cause?
Or blush to speak His name?[6]

---

1. *Education,* p. 253.

2. *Patriarchs and Prophets,* p. 553.

3. *Patriarchs and Prophets,* p. 151.

4. *Ibid.,* p. 153.

5. *Prophets and Kings,* p. 601.

6. Isaac Watts, "Am I A Soldier of the Cross?" *The Seventh-day Adventist Hymnal* (Hagerstown, Md.: Review and Herald Publishing Assn., 1985).

CHAPTER

Jesus Models Victory

The most significant battles fought in the great controversy involved the life and ministry of Christ on earth. In other instances examined thus far, we have noted Satan carrying out his war by proxies. He used other individuals or events to deceive God's people and lead them away from His priorities or cast doubt on His claims. But in the case of Jesus, the fight was often one on one: between Christ and Satan, particularly in the temptations in the wilderness, in Gethsemane, and on the cross. But in each case, Jesus won a decisive victory and showed how we, too, may win our war with Satan. Not in our own strength, for that can never be, but through complete reliance on Jesus.

The life of Jesus is a series of battles in the cosmic conflict between God and Satan. From the time of His incarnation, Satan tried every avenue, used every temptation, employed every means to abort the mission of Jesus, and thus thwart God's redemptive plan laid out before the foundation of the world. Satan "disputed every inch of advance in His path from the manger to Calvary."[1] He

> was exulting that he had succeeded in debasing the image of God in humanity. Then Jesus came to restore in man the image of his Maker. None but Christ can fashion anew the character that has been ruined by sin. He came to expel the demons that

had controlled the will. He came to lift us up from the dust, to reshape the marred character after the pattern of His divine character, and to make it beautiful with His own glory.[2]

In the fullness of time

"When the fullness of the time had come, God sent forth His Son, born of a woman, born under the law, to redeem those who were under the law, that we might receive the adoption as sons" (Galatians 4:4, 5). Nature moves with precision—from earth's orbit to atom's make-up. In the same way, God's purposes know no haste or delay. He operates with a strategy of exactness that includes the when and the how. When the divine clock strikes, He sets in motion His plans to fulfill His promises. In what sense did this fullness of time come?

The Incarnation was predetermined in the throne room of heaven (Isaiah 9:6), announced to Satan in Eden (Genesis 3:15), and timed by the prophecies of Daniel (Daniel 9:24, 25). In addition to these, the movement of history has come to a point where it was appropriate for God to reveal Himself.

> The world was at peace, under one government. Travel by land and sea was relatively safe and expeditious. There was a universal language, Greek. The Scriptures [Old Testament] had been available in Greek—the LXX [the Septuagint] for about two hundred years. Men were dissatisfied with their religious beliefs and were longing for the truth about life and human destiny. The Jews were dispersed everywhere, and in spite of themselves, bore witness to the true God. From all parts of the world they came to attend the feasts at Jerusalem, and could carry with them, as they returned, news of the Messiah's coming. Providence could have appointed no place and time more auspicious for launching the gospel message to the world than Palestine at this period in history.[3]

Satan, too, was aware of the time, and he was making the world ripe for darkness to rule. Under his leadership,

> sin had become a science, and vice was consecrated as a part of religion. Rebellion had struck its roots deep into the heart, and the hostility of man was most violent against heaven. It was

demonstrated before the universe that, apart from God, humanity could not be uplifted. A new element of life and power must be imparted by Him who made the world.[4]

So Jesus came. But at the very moment of His birth began Satan's assault on Him. If He could only dispose of Him physically, how easy his plans would have succeeded. The murderer from the beginning (John 8:44) did not hesitate to employ physical annihilation. Through the agent of a jealous and wicked governor, himself a part of God's chosen people, Satan tried to destroy the Baby Jesus along with all other innocent children.

At Bethlehem, "the hinge of history" turned in the great war between Christ and Satan. The Second Person of the Godhead stepped into human flesh in order to show to the universe that God is love, and His laws are just. He, as a human being, would be "obedient to the point of death, even the death of the cross" (Philippians 2:8). When it was all over, Satan would stand defeated, and "every tongue [including Satan's] should confess that Jesus is Lord, to the glory of God the Father" (Philippians 2:11).

Temptation in the wilderness

Born for a mission, commissioned to a task at the baptism, anointed by the Holy Spirit, Jesus retreated to the wilderness to contemplate the task ahead, the journey that He and He alone must traverse. How to fulfill God's mission? How to establish God's kingdom here on the enemy's territory? His strength was found in prayer, His assurance in God's mission. But the tempter was waiting for his moment to strike.

When the Savior was weak from forty days of fasting, when He seemed to stand alone, when the journey ahead looked bleak and weary, Satan took personal command in his attack against the Savior: "Satan saw that he must either conquer or be conquered. The issues of the conflict involved too much to be entrusted to his confederate angels. He must personally conduct the warfare."[5]

Satan struck with three fierce temptations. An appeal for Jesus to prove His divinity by satisfying hunger; a doubt of God's guiding hand over Him; and finally, an offer of the kingdoms of this earth for just a simple bow of worship to Satan. In each of these temptations, Jesus triumphed. What was the secret of Jesus' victory?

First, He had a sense of God's mission. Jesus took life seriously, and lived it in the context of His Father: " 'For I have come down from heaven, not to do My own will, but the will of Him who sent Me' " (John 6:38). From the very beginning of His ministry, Jesus was conscious that He was sent by the Father to do His will, to show that God's law is not arbitrary, to reveal that God is love, and to redeem fallen humanity from sin.

Nothing could deter Jesus from this sense of God's mission and purpose.

Satan was unwearied in his efforts to overcome the Child of Nazareth. From His earliest years Jesus was guarded by heavenly angels, yet His life was one long struggle against the powers of darkness. That there should be upon the earth one life free from the defilement of evil was an offense and a perplexity to the prince of darkness. He left no means untried to ensnare Jesus. No child of humanity will ever be called to live a holy life amid so fierce a conflict with temptation as was our Saviour.[6]

Armed with this sense of God's mission, Jesus withheld the fiercest of Satan's attack. The third temptation offered Jesus what He came to achieve, an opportunity to win back this planet for God, seemingly without any cost. He took Jesus to a mountaintop and showed Him all the kingdoms of the earth. He no longer used the bait, "If you are the Son of God," but instead offered the allurement of a crown without a cross. He said, "Why go through the struggles of sweat, blood, and God-forsakenness, and die on the cross? What assurance is there that at the end of it all, there will be the kingdom? Is not the Father self-centered and does He not spare Himself all the agony, and instead pass on the bitter cup for you to drink? That the Father did everything including the creation of human beings for His selfish pleasure—this has been my argument, the basis of my quarrel with Him. And now He sets you on death row, without any light at the end of the tunnel. But . . ."

That was a dangerous "but." Nevertheless, Satan pressed on the tired and lonely Jesus: " 'All these things I will give You if You will fall down and worship me' " (Matthew 4:9). The temptation was strong and fierce. But Jesus' defense was stronger than Satan's attack. His defense lay in an abiding sense of God's mission.

Second, Jesus relied upon God's Word. Knowing the Word is not enough. Satan quoted the Scriptures, but that was to cheat and defraud. The power of God's Word is available only when the soul unconditionally surrenders to the demands of that Word. Doubting God's Word is one sharp armor in Satan's arsenal of deception. He tried it successfully with Adam and Eve, and tried it again with the Second Adam, Jesus. Satan prefaced the first two temptations with a bait of self-doubt: "If you are the Son of God." Only a few days earlier, at the baptismal commission of Jesus, even as the Holy Spirit descended upon Jesus, God the Father proclaimed from heaven, " 'This is My beloved Son, in whom I am well pleased' " (Matthew 3:17).

Satan knew this. Yet at the moment of Jesus' greatest physical weakness, Satan appealed to Him to prove His divinity by turning stones into bread. But Jesus, fortified by God's Word, would neither doubt His divinity, nor exchange the Cross for a bakery. Likewise in the second temptation, Jesus refused to doubt God's Word or test Him on His promise of protection and safety. Faith that opts for its own self-test is no faith at all, and Jesus triumphed by throwing His lot on the divine mission and the divine Word.

> The Son of God was not to prove His divinity to Satan, or to explain the reason of His humiliation. By conceding to the demands of the rebel, nothing for the good of man or the glory of God would be gained. Had Christ complied with the suggestion of the enemy, Satan would still have said, Show me a sign that I may believe you to be the Son of God. Evidence would have been worthless to break the power of rebellion in his heart. And Christ was not to exercise divine power for His own benefit. He had come to bear trial as we must do, leaving us an example of faith and submission. Neither here nor at any subsequent time in His earthly life did He work a miracle in His own behalf.[7]

Jesus vanquished Satan by absolute reliance and confidence in God's Word. The way of Christ is neither sensational nor conditional—to make bread out of stone or to jump from the temple's pinnacle. The way of Christ is quiet trust in God's Word.

Third, Jesus maintained a close relationship with God. While a sense of divine mission kept His direction in focus, and reliance on God's Word provided Him a strength to bear every attack, it was His personal and continuous relationship with the Father that sustained Him in every battle of life.

There was in Him nothing that responded to Satan's sophistry. He did not consent to sin. Not even by a thought did He yield to temptation. So it may be with us. Christ's humanity was united with divinity; He was fitted for the conflict by the indwelling of the Holy Spirit. And He came to make us partakers of the divine nature. So long as we are united to Him by faith, sin has no more dominion over us. God reaches for the hand of faith in us to direct it to lay fast hold upon the divinity of Christ, that we may attain to perfection of character.[8]

The carrot of the kingdom of this world

Throughout Jesus' ministry, many hoped, some wanted, and a few pushed Him to be the king—the political, economic, and religious leader of the Jews—to throw the Romans out. His own brothers were upset with the direction of His ministry (John 7:3-5). Nathanael declared Him to be the King (John 1:49). John the Baptist doubted the effectiveness of Christ's ministry because he had not seen Him move to assert His royal authority (Matthew 11:2-6). Peter almost became Satan's spokesperson in denouncing Jesus' way of the Cross (Matthew 16:21-23). Matthew was one of the Zealots who believed in the violent overthrow of the Romans. Judas never ceased to question Jesus for failing to use His divine power to grasp the throne. And Satan, the master of Judas, tempted Jesus again and again with this option.

The times, when Jesus ministered, also supported an arrogant, violent, nationalism. Josephus the historian, tells of two instances.[9] One concerns Theudas who declared himself to be a prophet, and swayed thousands of Jews to follow him to the Jordan and watch him divide the waters. The Romans crushed him. The other concerns an Egyptian, a self-declared prophet, who led a crowd to the Mount of Olives. He claimed that at his word the walls of Jerusalem would collapse, and he would set up the kingdom. The Romans quelled this uprising too.

Against this background and in the context of the many miracles Jesus performed, particularly the one of feeding the 5,000 (John 6:5-13), is it any wonder that Satan held before the crowds the carrot of a temporal kingdom? And the mob was ready to seize Jesus and by force make Him a king (John 6:14,15).

Kingship was not at question in the mind of the Savior. When Pilate asked Him if He was the king of the Jews, Jesus did not deny, but only affirmed that

His " 'kingdom is not of this world' " (John 18:36). Jesus drew a line between two kingdoms: the political and the spiritual, the economic and the moral, the temporal and the eternal, and the visible and not-yet visible.

Given the fact that His kingdom is spiritual and not political, we must also note that Jesus did teach that the kingdom of God is already here, and that it is coming. It is both—a present reality and a future prospect, an experience as well as a hope. Some have found these sayings regarding the nature of God's kingdom confusing. However, "Jesus' message is that in his own person and mission God has invaded human history and has triumphed over evil, even though the final deliverance will occur only at the end of the age."[10]

The "already" settles the finality of the kingdom—-Christ has ushered it in history: "The kingdom of God's grace is now being established, as day by day hearts that have been full of sin and rebellion yield to the sovereignty of His love."[11] The "not yet" assures the physical end of evil and the establishment of the new earth. "The full establishment of the kingdom of His glory will not take place until the second coming of Christ to this world."[12] The one assures the other; and both balance each other.

The kingdom is here, with its victory over evil already a fact. But the whole creation is groaning and waiting for deliverance (Romans 8:22, 23), on that day when " 'the kingdoms of this world have become the kingdoms of our Lord and of His Christ, and He shall reign forever and ever!' " (Revelation 11:15). Both the kingdom of grace now and the kingdom of glory yet to come belong to Jesus. Being part of the first brings us final victory in the great controversy and entrance into the kingdom of glory.

---

1. *Selected Messages,*1:406, 407.

2. *The Desire of Ages,* pp. 37, 38.

3. *The SDA Bible Commentary,* 5:965.

4. *The Desire of Ages,* p. 37.

5. *Ibid.,* p. 116.

6. *Ibid.,* p. 71.

7. *Ibid.,* p. 119.

8. *Ibid.,* p. 123.

9. See *Antiquities,* xx.5.1; 8:6.

10. George E. Ladd, *A Theology of the New Testament* (Grand Rapids: William B. Eerdmans, 1974), p. 67.

11. *Thoughts From the Mount of Blessing,* p. 108.

12. *Ibid.*

CHAPTER

The Great Controversy in the Parables of Jesus

Jesus took simple stories from common everyday experiences or from incidents known to His hearers to teach great and precious gems of truth.

With Jesus a parable was a bridge by which He led His hearers by a pleasant and familiar path from where they were to where He wanted them to be, from the known to the unknown, from concrete facts to abstract truths, from the seen to the unseen, from the earthly to the heavenly. It was a window through which He invited His hearers to gaze upon vistas of heavenly truth.[1]

The Gospels record some forty parables. In many of these parables, Jesus taught the reality of the great controversy, the subtlety of Satan in deceiving men and women in this spiritual warfare, and how our decisions affect our role and status in the cosmic conflict. While we could trace the theme of the conflict between Christ and Satan in many of the parables, we will limit ourselves to considering five parables: the soils, the wheat and the tares, the vineyard, the wedding feast and the wedding garments, and the lost son.

The parable of the soils
In spite of Jesus' miracles and great revelations of truth, "the Phari-

sees went out and plotted against Him, how they might destroy Him" (Matthew 12:14). In every age, some accept the good news of Jesus and others reject it. Why does this happen?

Jesus provided an answer through the parable of the soils. " 'A sower went out to sow,' " begins the parable (Matthew 13:3). The sower had very good intentions. The seed was good. He sowed with care and much hope. But when the time came for germination, growth, and harvest, the results were not the same. Some seed fell by the wayside and the birds devoured them. Some fell on stony places, and the sun scorched and burnt the newly germinated plants. Some fell among the thorns and got choked by the harshness of the environment. But the seeds that fell on good ground yielded a multitude of harvest (Matthew 13:4-8).

This parable teaches that the germination and fruitbearing of the seed is dependent on the nature and receptivity of the soil. Where that receptivity and nurture are lacking, the seed does not yield its expected harvest. Jesus gave us some profound insights.

First, He said, " 'the wicked one comes and snatches away what was sown in his heart' " (Matthew 13:19). The devil attacks directly, but he has other subtle ways of preventing acceptance of truth and fruitbearing. Second, he prevents the seed from taking deep roots. Third, cares of the world may choke the Word. In every case, the intention of the evil one is the same: to prevent nurture and growth of the human soul in the kingdom of God. It is his plan to cloud the understanding and confuse the issues, so that God's Word will not yield the desired fruit.

As the birds are ready to catch up the seed from the wayside, so Satan is ready to catch away the seeds of divine truth from the soul. He fears that the word of God may awaken the careless, and take effect upon the hardened heart. Satan and his angels are in the assemblies where the gospel is preached. While angels of heaven endeavor to impress hearts with the word of God, the enemy is on the alert to make the word of no effect. With an earnestness equaled only by his malice, he tries to thwart the work of the Spirit of God. While Christ is drawing the soul by His love, Satan tries to turn away the attention of the one who is moved to seek the Saviour. He engages the mind with worldly schemes. He excites criticism, or insinuates doubt and unbelief.[2]

But Satan is never the winner in any absolute sense. He may deceive some here, some there, but the purpose of God will not come to naught. The parable is not one of despair, but one of hope. Against the wayside heart of rejection; against the stony heart of indecisiveness and indifference; against the heart filled with the thorns of the cares of this world and deceitfulness of riches; the gospel reaches the heart of the fertile soil as well. That heart knows its needs; reaches out to God's mercy and truth; receives the truth; and lets the sunshine and dew of the Holy Spirit bring forth a rich harvest—" 'some a hundredfold, some sixty, some thirty' " (Matthew 13:23).

"A knowledge of the truth depends not so much upon strength of intellect as upon pureness of purpose, the simplicity of an earnest, dependent faith. To those who in humility of heart seek for divine guidance, angels of God draw near. The Holy Spirit is given to open to them the rich treasures of the truth. The good-ground hearers, having heard the word, keep it. Satan with all his agencies of evil is not able to catch it away."[3]

What is the secret of the fertile soil? It is clinging to Jesus and seeking understanding from Him who is the Truth. It is letting the Holy Spirit abide in one's heart to bring the desired fruits. The outcome of the great controversy is in no doubt. God will have His harvest. Satan may deceive many, but he cannot take away the fulfillment of the good news of the gospel and the establishment of God's kingdom.

The parable of the wheat and tares

Here the soil was rich and fertile. The seed was good. With all the care, the sowing was done. But when the plants came up, the servants observed tares growing along with the wheat. In astonishment, they asked the farmer, " 'Did you not sow good seed in your field? How then does it have tares?' " (Matthew 13:27).

The parable of the wheat and the tares (Matthew 13:24-30) has a perennial truth. It confronts the mystery of evil and God's remedy for it. The answer to the servants' question is remarkable for its directness and clarity: " 'An enemy has done this' " (Matthew 13:28). The parable makes no attempt to deny the presence of wickedness and evil. To do so is diametrically opposed to the teaching of God's Word. Wickedness is not an illusion. It is not an immature action. It is not something that just happens. It is the act of the evil one. It is alien to the principles of God and intends to disrupt God's will and purpose. Christ draws the line between wheat and tares, between righteousness and sin. One is God's way, the other is Satan's way.

Every heart is a field in which good wheat is sown by the God of truth, but the evil one lingers around, and wants to let the tares grow and choke out the wheat. Did he not do this with Adam and Eve? Did not God create Adam and Eve without any propensity to evil? In the midst of such perfect and ideal conditions, Satan sowed the weed of sin. It is this conflict between the Sower of the wheat and the sower of the tares that this parable deals with.

Consider five implications from the parable. *First,* the presence of evil in this world owes its origin to the enemy. God cannot be held responsible, but God has made a provision as to how to deal with it. *Second,* the hindrance to the spread of the gospel and its acceptance must also be laid at the feet of the enemy. It is he who secretly and silently lets the tares grow and attempts to choke out the wheat. *Third,* within the fertile soil of the church there also exists the possibility of weeds growing up. Indeed, there is a real possibility that we may be like tares—but for the grace of God. Hence, *fourth,* while we must be ruthless with weeds in our own lives, we should not rush to judgment on others. Love and patience are graces that ought to govern our dealing with the tares, for not always are they easily visible, as in the case of this parable. The tares and the wheat are so similar that they cannot be distinguished until they come to the fruit-bearing stage. *Fifth,* God's control over the finality of the conflict between wheat and tares is never usurped. Satan tempts us to deal with tares in our midst so that the wheat, too, may be pulled up. But God's plan is different. He has reserved the fate of the tares till Judgment Day.

The teaching of this parable is illustrated in God's own dealing with men and angels. Satan is a deceiver. When he sinned in heaven, even the loyal angels did not fully discern his character. This was why God did not at once destroy Satan. Had He done so, the holy angels would not have perceived the justice and love of God. A doubt of God's goodness would have been as evil seed that would yield the bitter fruit of sin and woe. Therefore the author of evil was spared, fully to develop his character. Through long ages God has borne the anguish of beholding the work of evil, He has given the infinite Gift of Calvary, rather than leave any to be deceived by the misrepresentations of the wicked one; for the tares could not be plucked up without danger of uprooting the precious grain. And shall we not be as forbearing toward our fellow men as the Lord of heaven and earth is toward Satan?[4]

"An enemy has done this," said Jesus. The enemy does a lot in this world, in the church, in our homes, and in our lives. Each one is a battlefield in the great controversy. We ought to be aware of the presence of tares growing up. Our instant reaction to pull out the tares needs to be guarded. In our eagerness to implement what we consider truth and righteousness, we may pull out the wheat also.

> As the tares have their roots closely intertwined with those of the good grain, so false brethren in the church may be closely linked with true disciples. The real character of these pretended believers is not fully manifested. Were they to be separated from the church, others might be caused to stumble, who but for this would have remained steadfast.[5]

But this does not mean that the church should be slack in maintaining discipline within the fellowship. When sin is openly manifested, and immorality raises its head as "not even named among the Gentiles" (1 Corinthians 5:1), the church, must deal with it. But let it be with with kindness and love, lest any spirit of vengeance lead to the removal of the tender "wheat."

The parable of the wedding garment

A marriage feast at any level of society is an event of joy. But here (Matthew 22:1-14), we have a royal wedding. How much greater should the celebration be! But the invited ones " 'made light of it and went their ways' " (Matthew 22:5). The king provided everything for the feast. The best of food was there. The surroundings were befitting the royal status of the host. Even special clothing was made available to all the invitees.

The invitation was free, and all that needs to be done is for people to come. But they made "light" of the feast. Their self-interest was more important than the wedding feast of their king.

It is easy to apply the parable to the religious leaders of Christ's day who rejected God's invitation. But the parable points us to five significant elements in the great controversy, as God and Satan contend for our souls.

First, God's invitation to celebrate the joy of salvation. The invitation is free and is universal. It costs us nothing. All we need to do is accept it, and come to the feast of the Lord. But, like the children of Israel, we have our preoccupations—our work, business, family interests, personal enjoyment and pleasure. We have time for everything, except to come to God.

Second, God's persistence in inviting us. He is not weary. He is longing for all to come, and does not wish that any should be lost out of the joy of the wedding—and perish (2 Peter 3:9).

Third, human persistence in rejecting God's free offer of salvation. Often the rejection is not because of outright wickedness or even a refusal to recognize God. Satan is too cunning to do that, even though deliberate rejection is not out of his scheme. He works for human rejection by placing other preoccupations as priorities. The affairs of everyday life become more important than the urgency of listening to Jesus. Earning becomes more important than living. That is part of Satan's device in the cosmic conflict.

In his book, *The Screwtape Letters,* C. S. Lewis presents a series of imaginary letters that a senior demon, called Screwtape, writes to a junior partner not experienced in the skillful art of tripping human beings (especially the ones who consider themselves saints or on the verge of being so). In these letters, Screwtape gives detailed instruction as to how to divert people's attention from important issues, vital priorities, and appropriate concerns. For example, when John is praying for his mother who is suffering from rheumatism, Screwtape advises the junior demon not to cause John to lose faith in prayer. Instead, John should be encouraged to pray for his mother at all times. This strategy will divert John's attention from the necessity of massaging his mother's aching joints.

In another letter, Screwtape suggests that Christians must be encouraged to worry and fret over grave issues in order to divert their attention from immediate problems that confront their soul. The name of the game, says Screwtape, "is to have them all running about with fire extinguishers whenever there is a flood."

How often we become victims of the Screwtape technique and pat ourselves on the back that we are pretty good saints! We spend enormous time debating the minute points of a doctrine but hardly tell anyone that Jesus saves. We are so busy speaking of global mission that we can't cross the street in the name of Jesus. We are concerned about the movements of the body during worship hour, but hardly let our inmost beings be touched by the demands of that worship experience. We sing amazing grace, but trust in our inner strength. We preach God's saving grace, but refuse to come to His wedding feast.

Fourth, God's feast of joy will not go unattended. If people do not accept the gospel just as the Jews of Christ's day, that does not mean the failure of the gospel. The wedding feast will go on. From the highways and the byways—the most unexpected places—guests will come and fill the wedding hall. But coming itself is not enough. The coming requires certain appropriateness. The parable informs us that the king came to inspect the guests and found one who did not have the proper garment (Matthew 22:11). He had refused to wear the special garment that the King Himself had provided. That is another form of rejecting the King. Satan's game is simply to convince you to be your own person, wear your own clothes, and assert yourself. But you cannot accept the King and refuse His conditions at the same time. That leads to the next point.

Fifth, God's invitation is free, but He expects those who come to do His bidding. The bidding is not burdensome. He wants his guests to wear the appropriate garment He Himself provides.

> Only the covering which Christ Himself has provided can make us meet to appear in God's presence. This covering, the robe of His own righteousness, Christ will put upon every repenting, believing soul. "I counsel thee," He says, "to buy of Me . . . white raiment, that thou mayest be clothed, and that the shame of thy nakedness do not appear." Rev. 3:18. This robe, woven in the loom of heaven, has in it not one thread of human devising. Christ in His humanity wrought out a perfect character, and this character He offers to impart to us.[6]

Without the garment of Christ's righteousness, we are lost (Matthew 22:12, 13). Self-righteousness saves no one.

The parable of the lost son

Luke 15 is a portrayal of the lost condition of humanity. That lost condition began in Eden as soon as the great controversy entered the human arena. What causes this lost condition in humans? Like the parable of the coin, some may be lost without knowing that they are lost. Like the lost sheep, some may wander away from the fold and get lost in the wilderness of no divine care. But it is the lost son that must occupy our attention. He gets lost deliberately, willfully, and selfishly.

In all the three stories of being "lost," one singular fact emerges: the importance of "one" in the eyes of God. God's love is so vast, so amazing, that He would empty heaven in order to find the one lost coin, one lost sheep, and one lost son. Christianity, above all other religions, openly declares the worth of one single individual. All the treasures in the home may be priceless, but the one lost coin needs to be searched for and found. The ninety-nine sheep provide some comfort to the shepherd, but he must seek after the one lost sheep in the darkness of the night and peril of the wilderness.

Every person is distinct in their own way. There is no one like me. Search the world. Look through history. Research the mysteries of biology or physiology. Turn to psychology or psychoanalysis. There is no one like me. Like my fingerprint. Like my voice or thought or failings or fulfillment. I am me. Even in sin, there is none like me. Jesus gave notice to Satan that He has come to seek and save me. "If there had been but one lost soul, Christ would have died for that one."[7] I, as an individual, am that precious to God.

The parable of the lost son (Luke 15:11-32) focuses sharply on the issues in the great controversy.

First, consider the love of the father. It doesn't take much imagination to see how much the father must have pled when the younger son made his demand. That portion of the estate was his, but must estate or riches or even longing for the distant land disrupt the relationship between the father and the son? The father saw in the son's demand an impending break in their relationship, but the son saw his freedom to be what he wanted to be. There lies the ache of love and the indifference of self-seeking. In the context of the great controversy, we can imagine the scene back in eternity when God pleaded with Lucifer with longings of love, and Lucifer rebelled against God. He had an eye on the "mountain of God" as if that mount could be his. The distant land may have its charms, but not worth rupturing the love relationship with the Father.

Second, consider the role of self in the decision of the younger son. The sin of the son began with self-assertion: *"Give me."* He didn't care about his father's love, the safety of the home, or the uncertainties of the distant land. All that mattered was self-will, and self-will is the destroyer of the best in life. Families, churches, friendships, and even one's destiny can fall victim on the altar of self-worship. Self-indulgence has but one terminus—the distant land, away from home.

But is the beauty of life as God created in the human being. He may be a prodigal son, but he is a son nevertheless. Within his soul was flickering a dim and latent light of the image of God. He looked at the pigs, then looked at himself—how low he had sunk—and his heart throbbed back to the heart of the father. So he asked himself the question: *Why me?*

When self realizes its folly and repents of its evil and is willing to come down from the throne upon which it has placed itself, hope arises. Why should I be in the midst of these pigs? Why should I starve? Why should I be a nameless creature, lost in the distant land? No devil can force one to take the path of sin and God cannot force one to take the path of repentance. Self must choose, either way. So the young man, rose to go back home, with a ready speech, full of contrition, seeking mercy and forgiveness (Luke 15:18-21).

Between the wastefulness of sin and the beauty of restoration, the young man saw the folly of his choice and the unfailing love of the Father. The prodigality that started with a *"Give me"* now turns to repentance with a *"Make me."* Self-assertion is gone. Self-abandonment opens the door of hope. The return to the father was a return to his love, to his mercies. "Make me a servant," he pleaded after confessing that he had sinned against heaven. Every self-willed action is a sin against heaven, and only thereafter it is a sin against an individual. Make me whatever you will. The confession came from a realization of his own unworthiness (Luke 15:21).

Salvation does not come because we are worthy. It comes to those who realize their unworthiness and turn to God's grace. It comes only when self is surrendered. The restoration of the younger son not only teaches the dangerous road of self-will, but also the unfailing love of the Father.

Third, realize the folly of the older brother. The younger son had to learn the nature of the Father's love and the mistaken grandeur of self-will. But the older son did not learn that lesson at all, even though he remained home. *"You never gave me,"* was his charge against his father. He was with his father, but did not know him. His was a self-centeredness of another kind: a smug self-satisfaction called religion. Good religion. Self-righteous religion. Religion that sought to earn the love of the father through its own good works.

Wearing the cloak of religion, living in a home called church, one could grow up not knowing the power or the purpose of God's love. Satan delights in either kind of self-will. In the context of the great controversy, it is so important that we follow the example of the apostle and die daily (1 Corinthians 15:31).

---

1. *The SDA Bible Dictionary* (Hagerstown, Md.: Review and Herald Pub. Assn., 1979), p. 835.

2. *Christ's Object Lessons,* pp. 44, 45.

3. *Ibid.,* p. 59.

4. *Ibid.,* p. 72.

5. *Ibid.*

6. *Ibid.,* p. 311.

7. *Ibid.,* p. 187.

CHAPTER

The Great Controversy and the Miracles of Jesus

A miracle is a supernatural event that cannot be understood or explained according to known natural law. Our limitations in knowledge and understanding do not permit an explanation for such events that take place as a result of divine intervention in human affairs. If we concede, as we ought to from an understanding of what the Bible says, that God is Omniscient and Omnipotent, then God can perform the miracle when and as He chooses.

The New Testament records some thirty-five miracles Jesus performed. Most of these involved healing the sick. Each one was performed for a specific purpose—to fulfill a human need, to glorify God, to reveal that He was sent from God, or to reveal some aspect of spiritual truth (Mark 2:9-11; John 6:11, 12; 9:3-7).

The Gospels also record many instances when Jesus refused to perform a miracle, although He could have. He did not respond to Satan's demand for a miracle in the wilderness. He did not rescue Himself from the suffering He faced in Gethsemane or at the Cross.

Why did not Jesus perform a miracle on these occasions? The answer points to one of the great christological principles in the New Testament. To Jesus, miracles were the means to fulfill the will of God and not to meet His own needs. He came to fight the devil on his turf, as an example to the rest of humanity, and He would not employ any of His divine power to overcome the devil or to derive any personal benefit.

However, both the miracles Jesus did not perform and the ones He did perform were to advance the mission of His Father on earth. They gave notice to Satan that His defeat in the great controversy is certain. To that extent, the miracles show how closely they are related to Christ's role and eventual victory in the cosmic conflict between good and evil.

By the pool of Bethesda

The pool of Bethesda in Jerusalem was known for miracles. Around the pool lay broken pieces of clay in the form of "a great multitude of sick people, blind, lame, paralyzed" (John 5:3). They all waited for the strange stirring of the water for hope to become a reality. Whoever jumped into the waters at the time of the stirring was healed of whatever malady afflicted them. Near that pool, one particular man comes to our attention. His name is not given. He is a forgotten person, given up for no good by his family and everyone else. He has no friends. With a streak of sadness, he says, " 'I have no man [to help]' " (John 5:7).

Every time he tried to jump into the pool, someone beat him to it. He was weak and broken, but a man with great hope. For thirty-eight years he hoped, and today that hope will be realized. Today will be his day of salvation.

Jesus stopped by. And where Jesus is, there is hope. The meeting of the two—the Creator and this broken and helpless man—brought about a miracle that defied the laws of nature. The faith of the man in Jesus brought the Savior to his rescue. " 'Take up your bed and walk,' " commanded Jesus (John 5:8).

> The man's faith takes hold upon that word. Every nerve and muscle thrills with new life, and healthful action comes to his crippled limbs. Without question he sets his will to obey the command of Christ, and all his muscles respond to his will. Springing to his feet, he finds himself an active man. Jesus had given him no assurance of divine help. The man might have stopped to doubt, and lost his one chance of being healed. But he believed Christ's word, and in acting upon it he received strength.[1]

While the miracle produced joy for the sick man and an opportunity for Jesus to affirm His equality with the Father, it also aroused anger among the Jews because Jesus performed the miracle on Sabbath. Satan used this moment of mercy as a battle against Christ in the continuing struggle of the great controversy. "He would lead them to reject Christ and to make His life as bitter as possible, hoping to discourage Him in His mission. And the leaders in Israel became instruments of Satan in warring against the Saviour."[2]

Note how in this miracle Satan tried to advance his cause in the ongoing battle. He incited Jewish leaders to accuse Jesus of breaking the law because He did the healing on Sabbath. How ironic! The Law-Giver was accused of breaking the law by those who claimed to be trustees of the law, when all that the Law-Giver did was to redeem the man lost to the consequences of sin. The open clash on Sabbath was not fought on the need for Sabbath, but on the core purpose of God's law—showing that God's law is the law of love. Satan is content as long as we remain faithful to the routines of religion, while forgetting the core of religious experience of faithful discipleship.

Jesus responded to the Jewish leaders by claiming equality with the Father and by asserting that He was doing exactly what God the Father has been doing. He placed His mission of mercy as part of fulfilling the law. "Heaven's work never ceases, and men should never rest from doing good . . . The work of Christ in healing the sick was in perfect accord with the law. It honored the Sabbath."[3]

Through this miracle, Jesus brought the grace of God and the needs of humanity and showed how human need can be met. "Sin no more," Jesus commanded the healed man. A redeemed person walks no more in sin. A redeemed person continues to claim God's grace and walks in obedience to His law. The miracle by the pool is one more victory in the cosmic conflict, uplifting God's grace and upholding His law.

The centurion's servant

Here is a miracle in contrasts (Matthew 8:5-13). The centurion was a Roman military authority, under whom 100 soldiers served. He implemented the will of Caesar. His word was the law—it carried authority and demanded immediate implementation. He was someone to be feared and served. If this officer came to Jesus and asked for the healing of his son, that would be normal. But his mission was on behalf of his slave—a bond slave. The Roman culture and society did not consider a slave a human being. A slave was just an "it"—a tool to do a job. But this centurion and his slave seemed to have come together in their search for divine grace and healing. The centurion's attitude was in harmony with the gospel's purpose to break down barriers dividing humanity.

Wherever there is division—ethnic, linguistic, color, tribal, or caste—it brings dishonor to God's cause and plays into Satan's hand. While the centurion showed the spirit of the gospel in the embrace of grace and concern he had for his slave, observe the attitude of the Jews. They were surprised that Jesus offered to go to the home of the centurion, for they disapproved of a Jew going to the home of a Gentile (Matthew 8:7). Here were a people through whom all nations were to be blest, according to God's covenant with Abraham, and they would have nothing to do with Romans and Gentiles. They played straight into Satan's game of preventing the grace of God ever reaching the peoples of the world. But Christ came to counteract this devise of Satan. In Him and through Him, He creates a common humanity without any dividing wall.

Jesus offered to go to the Roman's home. But the officer's faith in the healing power of the Savior was astounding—even to Jesus Himself. *First, the centurion says he is unworthy to receive Jesus into his home* (Matthew 8:8). The miracle of God's grace begins there—recognition of one's unworthiness. In the cosmic conflict, Satan would have men and women affirm their self-importance and their self-worth. But the real winner in the battle is one who recognizes that his or her worth lies not in themselves, but in God's grace. That was the difference between Cain and Abel. That was the difference in this miracle between the Jewish leaders and the Gentile centurion.

Second, the officer said, " 'Speak a word, and my servant will be healed' " (Matthew 8:8).

Trust in God's Word is our immediate and powerful weapon to carry the battle against the onslaughts of Satan. Whether it is resisting sin, fleeing a temptation, asking for a miracle, or removing deficiency, turn to the Word. There is power in it. While we cannot see God face to face, we have access to Him through His Word and prayer. The One who spoke and it was done at the Creation is still in our midst. His Word is here—and that is our weapon to fight the devil.

Jesus responded to the officer and immediately his slave was healed. Through this miracle, Christ provided afresh the meaning of God's kingdom—not an exclusive monopoly of a few, as Satan would want to have it with his eyes on the cosmic conflict. God's kingdom is an all-inclusive family, a rainbow of many colors. All that is needed to come into that kingdom is faith in God's saving grace.

The touch of faith

For twelve years Satan kept this woman (Mark 5:25-34) a captive to an incurable hemorrhage that weakened her body, burdened her mind, and isolated her spirit. She went to every physician, spent all that she had but in vain. Her captivity was so strong that she nearly lost hope. Satan's grip over humanity is strong, but is it strong enough to resist the power that comes from One who came to liberate humanity from the devil's clutches? This miracle says, "No."

The Gospel writer says that this woman heard of Jesus (Mark 5:27). Before Jesus healed this woman, He had performed at least sixteen miracles. Some of these miracles involved the poor, the unclean, the Gentiles, and women. None of them hoped to live a normal, useful life until they found Jesus. Is it possible that someone had told this woman about what Jesus had done and could do? Spreading the good news about Jesus is among the first steps to take in defeating the purposes of Satan.

But hearing about Jesus is not enough. Knowledge never saves anyone. Knowing must lead to faith, and faith must lead to coming, and coming must lead to touching Jesus—be part of Him. That journey, this woman risked to take. " 'If only I may touch His clothes, I shall be made well' " (Mark 5:28).

Her faith was a risk because of two reasons. First, Jewish custom had excluded women from many privileges that men enjoyed. An orthodox Jew would include in his daily prayers three things for which he was thankful. He would pray every morning, "Lord, I thank You that You have not made me a slave. Lord, I thank You that you have not made me a Gentile. Lord, I thank You that You have not made me a woman." Against that kind of atmosphere, this woman dared to touch Jesus and risked her place in the community. Second, her disease was one that was considered by the Jewish custom as "unclean." Such an unclean person was expected to isolate herself. The fellowship of her father, the embrace of her brothers, the joy of a normal home and society were excluded from her. The "uncleanness" destined her to an isolated, depressive, and hopeless world for twelve, long years.

But her faith took the risk. " 'Whoever comes to me I will never drive away' " (John 6:37, NIV) is Christ's promise. Claiming that promise and armed with a faith that could not be shaken, the woman approached Jesus, touched the hem of His garment, and was instantly healed. There was no miracle in either her touch or His clothes. The miracle must be located in her faith, as Jesus Himself said, " 'Daughter, your faith has made you well. Go in peace, and be healed of your affliction' " (Mark 5:34).

Genuine faith brings heaven's resources to the aid of the needy sinner. Divine rescue in the cosmic conflict is only a touch away. Jesus asked, "Who touched Me?" The question is not one of rebuke, but recognition that only in the faith that touches God and stays close to Him there is safety and refuge from the onslaughts of Satan. We cannot be victorious in spiritual warfare unless we have that kind of faith.

> To talk of religion in a casual way, to pray without soul hunger and living faith, avails nothing. A nominal faith in Christ, which accepts Him merely as the Saviour of the world, can never bring healing to the soul. The faith that is unto salvation is not a mere intellectual assent to the truth.... It is not enough to believe about Christ; we must believe in Him. The only faith that will benefit us is that which embraces Him as a personal Saviour; which appropriates His merits to ourselves. Many hold faith as an opinion. Saving faith is a transaction by which those who receive Christ join themselves in covenant relation with God. Genuine faith is life. A living faith means an increase of vigor, a confiding trust, by which the soul becomes a conquering power.[4]

Faith—true faith—has the power to arrest God, to stop Him and make Him take note of a single person. He brings not only healing, but also liberation from Satan, and makes one a child of God. "Daughter," is the way Jesus addressed this unfortunate woman. It is an affectionate word. It is a word of transforming love. It is an inclusive word. No longer in despair, no longer in pain, faith transformed that woman into a child of the family of God.

Healing is good and is something we can pray for in faith. But not all prayers for healing receive such instant blessing. In an evangelistic meeting in India, as is the custom there, at the close of each night's preaching session, people came for special prayer—some for healing, others for spiritual strength, still others for a job or for passing an examination. I remember one night a woman brought her polio-stricken child. We prayed every day. We fasted and prayed. After three weeks of praying, there was no change in the child. But one night, the mother said, "I have already received the answer." "How come," I asked. "Pastor," she said, "you showed from the Word of God tonight that a day is coming and coming soon when Jesus will return, and on that day 'the lame shall leap like a deer, and the tongue of the dumb sing' (Isaiah 35:6). I am going to wait for that day even as I pray for God's love and care today and here."

That kind of faith provides victory in the great controversy.

"Lazarus, come forth"

The raising of Lazarus (John 11:1-45) reveals both the reality of death and the power of Jesus over death. It is one miracle, above all others, that established Christ as the Truth and the Life over and against Satan's opposing claims.

Since the first death that marked God's creation, death has been the lot of humanity—a result of sin. But death shall die at the hands of the Life-Giver, who Himself came to this world to conquer death and make eternal life available to all. The resurrection of Lazarus is a divine judgment against death, and a divine proclamation that all who will claim Jesus as their Friend shall live, even though they may die.

Note three important truths.

First, Jesus described the death of Lazarus as sleep (John 11:11). In so describing, Jesus was not simply waxing poetic. Nearly sixty-six times in seventeen books, the Bible uses sleep as the figure of speech to describe death. And when Jesus authenticated such usage, He established two significant realities: the unconscious state of the dead and the certainty of their waking up either for judgment or for eternal life. In the final events of earth's history—as part of God's process of cleansing the earth of sin and its consequences, and the establishment of a new heaven and earth—God will raise the dead.

Jesus grieved over death. The Lord knows what a painful experience death is. Even though death is a defeated foe in Jesus, it brings pain to those who experience it. "Jesus wept" (John 11:35), records the Bible. Days before Lazarus died, Mary and Martha had sent Him the message that their brother was gravely ill, and if He could only come, the curse of lingering death would pass away and the freshness of life would once more smile on Lazarus's face. As part of the emerging community of faith, the valiant three of Bethany believed and affirmed that Jesus was God in the flesh, that He held the keys of death and life, and that He was Israel's long-awaited Messiah.

Now death had snatched away one of the three. Jesus stood before the grave, surveyed the grieving and curious crowd, consoled the inconsolable Mary and Martha, and identified Himself with the grief of humanity. He wept.

Jesus commanded the dead to rise. But after the weeping came the command, " 'Lazarus, come forth!' " (John 11:43). The raising of Lazarus is not just a beautiful story. It is a reality check on human nature and death. It answers the question of what happens after death. It speaks of the hope of resurrection. It presents the One in whom alone is eternal life.

Until Jesus commanded Lazarus to come forth, he remained dead, unconscious, and in the grave. Martha had a problem with obeying the command of Jesus to roll away the stone. Her fear of the stench rivaled her faith in the resurrection.

Yes, resurrection is not an easy doctrine to believe. Satan does everything to obscure the promise. But Jesus was saying to Martha, "Why should you doubt in regard to My power? Why reason in opposition to My requirements? You have My word. If you will believe, you shall see the glory of God. Natural impossibilities cannot prevent the work of the Omnipotent One."[5]

The stone was removed, and Jesus issued the command. The voice of the Life-Giver penetrated the tomb. Life reversed the process of decay. The power of resurrection crushed the power of death. Lazarus came out, a witness to the authenticity of One who said to Martha, " 'I am the resurrection and the life. He who believes in Me, though he may die, he shall live. And whoever lives and believes in Me shall never die' " (John 11:25, 26).

Resurrection is thus God's answer to the problem of death. Christians must face death not by deluding themselves with the fictitious doctrine of the immortality of the soul, but by resting in the divine assurance of resurrection. There is no riddle or magic in this message. The Creator who brought the human being into existence can also resurrect that same being. It is as simple as that.

Look at the Cross again. There you see God's answer to the problem of sin. There you see the ultimate enemy vanquished by the blood of the sinless Son of God. There lies reconciliation and the hope of eternal life. And from there comes the assurance and the challenge, " 'I am the resurrection and the life. He who believes in Me, though he may die, he shall live. And whoever lives and believes in Me shall never die. Do you believe this?' " (John 11:25, 26).

Do we? Dare we not? Upon our choice rests our victory in the cosmic conflict.

---

1. *The Desire of Ages*, pp. 202, 203.
2. *Ibid.*, pp. 205, 206.
3. *Ibid.*, p. 207.
4. *Ibid.*, p. 347.
5. *Ibid.*, p. 535.

CHAPTER

Jesus
Wins the Victory

The cross of Jesus is at the center of God's plan to crush the revolt that erupted in heaven. It is the instrument of God's grace whereby sin is defeated and redemption is made available to all those who believe and accept Christ as their Savior.

From the age of twelve, Jesus was conscious of His Father's business and made that the paramount priority of His life and teachings (Luke 2:41-50). He taught, healed, and ministered with an inward compulsion to fulfill a predetermined mission for which His Father had sent Him to this world. Jesus was also fully aware that the mission involved His death as an atonement for sin and His resurrection as the final seal of God's triumph over Satan (Mark 8:31, 32).

With the vision of the Cross never fading or failing, Jesus lived in full anticipation of fulfilling the promise of the Creator in Genesis 3:15. He would crush the head of Satan. The outcome of the cosmic conflict between the forces of good and evil, between Christ and Satan, would be finally decided on the cross. Toward that objective Christ walked alone through the perils of the journey, the Last Supper, Gethsemane, and the Cross. At the end, the empty tomb affirmed His ultimate victory.

The journey to the Cross

Did Jesus have a certain sense of inevitability about the Cross? At least eight times in the Gospels, the word "must" is used in relationship to the sufferings and death of Jesus. He must go to Jerusalem. He must suffer. He must be rejected. He must be lifted up, and so on. The Cross was not an option to Jesus. It was a must. It was God's way of vindicating His character of love and the unchangeable nature of His law. In heaven Satan charged that God's law is arbitrary and His love is not absolute. The Cross would show that instead of changing the law, God sent forth His only Son to die on the cross as an atonement for sin.

Nothing would deter the Son of God from taking that journey to the Cross. He denounced any suggestion that He must have nothing to do with the Cross (Matthew 16:23). To Jesus, the journey to the Cross was not an option. It was a "must."

Remembering the Cross

Jesus knew that He must suffer and die, but to ensure that His disciples in generations to come remember the why of His death, He instituted the Communion service hours before He was betrayed. Jesus linked that service to the Passover (Matthew 26:17-19) and the image of the sacrificial lamb completed the historic time line from Eden to the Cross. He thus declared Himself as the Fulfillment of the covenant of Genesis 3:15. The Lord of history:

> took bread, blessed and broke it, and gave it to the disciples and said, "Take, eat; this is My body." Then He took the cup, and gave thanks, and gave it to them, saying, "Drink from it, all of you. For this is My blood of the new covenant, which is shed for many for the remission of sins" (Matthew 26:26-28).

Jesus' assertion that, through His broken body and shed blood He was establishing a new covenant (Matthew 26:28; 1 Corinthians 11:25), drives at the very core issue in the great controversy. Satan's charge in heaven is that God's law is arbitrary, unjust, and cannot be kept. This accusation had already been disproved in the sinless life of Jesus. Now with His own death, Jesus was establishing a new covenant by which the law will be written in the hearts of God's people (Jeremiah 31:31-34). The new covenant, flowing out of the Cross, enables us to love the Lord supremely and obey the commandments of Him "who gave Himself for our sins, that He might deliver us from this present evil age" (Galatians 1:4). Because of this, deliverance is ours in the great controversy.

Preparing for the Cross

Jesus prepared for the Cross in Gethsemane. It was perhaps one of the significant battlefields of the great controversy. Would the will and plan of God triumph over the calculated design of Satan to crush the Son of God? The design was already clear: rejection of Jesus by His own people; the indifference of the sleeping disciples; the planned betrayal by one and the expected denial by another; and the shadow of the Cross.

Jesus had still another greater agony to bear:

> He felt that by sin He was being separated from His Father. The gulf was so broad, so black, so deep, that His spirit shuddered before it. This agony He must not exert His divine power to escape. As man He must suffer the consequences of man's sin. As man He must endure the wrath of God against transgression. ... As the substitute and surety for sinful man, Christ was suffering under divine justice. ... He feared that in His human nature He would be unable to endure the coming conflict with the powers of darkness.[1]

Jesus sought strength in prayer, and even in that prayer, there was submission to God's will: "Not My will, but Yours." The bitter cup of the Cross was His to bear, but was there a way for the bitterness or the cup to disappear?

> The awful moment had come—that moment which was to decide the destiny of the world. The fate of humanity trembled in the balance. Christ might even now refuse to drink the cup apportioned to guilty man. It was not yet too late. He might wipe the bloody sweat from His brow, and leave man to perish in his iniquity. He might say, Let the transgressor receive the penalty of his sin, and I will go back to My Father.[2]

Nothing would have prevented Christ from going back to the Father, but what would have happened to the great controversy between God and Satan? Jesus took the eternal perspective and saw from eternity to eternity, and made His choice. He would submit Himself to drink the bitter cup and climb Golgotha. In such submission, we find the secret of victory.

Jesus Wins the Victory

The victory on the cross

The Cross is central to God's plan of defeating Satan in the great controversy. Without it, the universe would not have learned the true nature of rebellion in heaven. Without it, the problem of sin would not have been solved.

Look up to the Man on the cross—the Man Jesus—as He stays suspended between heaven and earth, in agony wondering whether the darkness of separation from the Father would be eternal as a result of His bearing the burden of sin in all its weight. Would He even now climb down, as Satan enticed Him to do? No. The Son of man has set His mind to break the shackles of sin forever, crush the evil one once and for all. He drinks the cup of the eternal covenant made long ago in the council halls of God's throne room, and cries out, " 'It is finished!' " (John 19:30). The task He had come to fulfill is done. Redemption from sin is accomplished. Reconciliation of the human race is completed. The evil one is crushed.

The Cross was not simply a tragedy. It was not an unfortunate incident in the life of a good man. It was not even martyrdom. It was the final revelation of God's love to man. It was God's way of showing that His law is just, His love is real, and He would save those who trust and follow Him. As we view the Cross, we must discover several basic truths that affect our lives in the spiritual warfare.

First, the Cross reveals to us God's character. Lucifer argued in heaven that God is an arbitrary ruler, with a law that cannot be kept. The Cross, however, shows the universe the true character of God: that He is not only gracious and merciful, but that He is love in the fullest sense of the word. "But God demonstrates His own love toward us, in that while we were still sinners, Christ died for us" (Romans 5:8).

> The more we study the divine character in the light of the cross, the more we see mercy, tenderness, and forgiveness blended with equity and justice, and the more clearly we discern innumerable evidences of a love that is infinite and a tender pity surpassing a mother's yearning sympathy for her wayward child.[3]

Second, the Cross reveals the unchangeable nature of God's law. If the law could have been changed, Jesus need not have died. But the law is as unchangeable as its Author that God let His Son bear the penalty of the transgression of the law, and by His sinless life and death showed to the universe that the law is unchangeable and that it can be obeyed.

> God did not change His law, but He sacrificed Himself, in Christ, for man's redemption. . . . The law requires righteousness,—a righteous life, a perfect character; and this man has not to give. He cannot meet the claims of God's holy law. But Christ, coming to the earth as man, lived a holy life, and developed a perfect character. These He offers as a free gift to all who will receive them. His life stands for the life of men.[4]

Third, the Cross makes us realize who we are. When Jesus cried from the cross, " 'Father, forgive them, for they do not know what they do' " (Luke 23:34), He was expressing an undeniable and universal truth. The first and foremost problem with humans is that we do not know ourselves. In our ignorance of what human life is, we ignore the supremacy of God. We violate the principles of nature. We confuse love with lust, self with God, means with goals, and beauty with butchery. We live in a world of our own, made of selfishness.

The Cross cries out: Enough!

Jesus climbed up that instrument of shame for you and me. He placed so much value on what we are worth, that He was willing to go down to the gutters of history and pick us up and place us under the sunshine of God's love. Before the Cross we discover our value, our dignity, and our worth. The Man on the cross would have gone there to save one single individual—just me, if I were the only sinner in the universe. The Cross has a singular message to give: God so loved me as a person that He gave me His only Son so that I might not perish but have everlasting life. At the Cross, I receive a sense of dignity and worth that the Creator has placed upon me—a worth that I dare not let Satan take away from me.

The Cross tells me that in this world where the great controversy is fought, I am a winner through the grace of Christ. I am a new person.

Fourth, the Cross offers forgiveness of sin. The apostle tells us: "The blood of Jesus Christ His Son cleanses us from all sin" (1 John 1:7). To lose the reality of the blood of Jesus shed on the cross in theology, proclamation, personal experience, or to teach that there is no such thing as the substitutionary act involved in the Cross, is to deny the divine origin and purpose of the Cross. It is also to walk into the trap that Satan has so well laid to make the Cross of no effect.

On the night before He was crucified, Jesus gave a solemn message to His disciples that they need to remember for ages to come. The bread and the wine are symbols of His body about to be broken and His blood about to be shed for the remission of sins (Matthew 26:28). The broken body and the shed blood were not acts of a martyr, suffering and dying for the vindication of His life or faith. Jesus was not a Lincoln, dying for the preservation of a nation and the liberation of a people. He was not a Gandhi dying for the overthrow of an alien bondage or for the emergence of a nation. Jesus was God's redemptive action for the problem of sin. Jesus asserted that His blood was to be " 'poured out for many for the forgiveness of sins' " (Matthew 26:28, NIV).

That shedding of the blood is crucial for the experience and appreciation of salvation. For one thing, it speaks about sin. Sin is real. Sin is costly. Sin's grip is so immense and deadly that forgiveness of sin and freedom from its power and guilt are impossible without the "precious blood of Christ" (1 Peter 1:19). This truth about sin needs to be said again and again because we live in a world that denies the reality of sin or remains indifferent to it. Vivekananda, the Hindu philosopher, once said that, "it is a sin to call a man a sinner. It is a standing libel on human nature."[5] That may well be the view of many today—from the materialist who defines life's occupation in terms of possession to the philosophic humanist who captures life's pursuit in terms of self-fulfillment. However, at the cross of Jesus we are confronted with the diabolical nature of sin, which can be crushed only by that blood " 'poured out for many for the forgiveness of sins' " (Matthew 26:28, NIV).

We are not saved by Christ the Good Man, by Christ the God-Man, by Christ the Great Teacher, or by Christ the Impeccable Example. We are saved by the Christ of the Cross:

> Christ was treated as we deserve, that we might be treated as He deserves. He was condemned for our sins, in which He had no share, that we might be justified by His righteousness, in which we had no share. He suffered the death which was ours, that we might receive the life which was His. "With His stripes we are healed."[6]

Any doctrine or practice or profession that diminishes or detracts from the centrality of the Cross cannot come from the One who said, " 'This cup is the new covenant in my blood; [Do this], in remembrance of me' " (1 Corinthians 11:25, NIV). Such doctrine must come from Satan who would delight to diminish the centrality of the Cross in the great controversy.

Fifth, the Cross brings about reconciliation. The Cross is God's instrument of effecting humanity's reconciliation with Him. "God was in Christ," says the apostle Paul, "reconciling the world to himself" (2 Corinthians 5:19). Because of what He did on the cross, I am able to stand before God without sin and without fear.

Reconciliation with God immediately opens up the second phase of the process: reconciliation with our fellow humans. One of the beautiful pictures I see at the cross is the variety of people crowded around there. Not all were admirers of Jesus. Not all were saints. There were Egyptians who prided themselves in their business acumen.

There were Romans who boasted in their civilization and culture. There were Greeks who excelled in their learning. There were Jews who considered themselves as God's chosen people. There were Pharisees who thought they were the chosen of the chosen and Sadducees who thought they were doctrinally pure. There were slaves who sought freedom and free men who indulged in the luxury of leisure. There were men, women, and children.

The Cross made no distinction between all these. It judged all of them as sinners. It offered to all of them the divine path of reconciliation. At the foot of the cross the ground is level. Human and human are brought together—nothing divides them anymore. A new brotherhood is launched. A new fellowship begins. East merges with west, north comes down to south, white shakes hands with black, rich leaps over to clasp the poor. The Cross bids all to the fountain of the blood—to taste the sweetness of life, to share the experience of grace, and to proclaim to the world the creation of a new rainbow of God's family.

The Cross restores what was lost in Eden—both the vertical relationship with God and the horizontal relationship with each other.

Sixth, the Cross expects death of self. Sin began with self-will. Christ who died for our sins expects us to crucify our self and live a life of obedience. You cannot read the New Testament without coming to grips with this fundamental aspect, of the new life in Christ. Read Galatians 2:20, "I have been crucified with Christ; it is no longer I who live, but Christ lives in me;

and the life which I now live in the flesh I live by faith in the Son of God, who loved me and gave Himself for me." Or read Romans 6:6, 11: "Our old man was crucified with Him, that the body of sin might be done away with, that we should no longer be slaves of sin. . . . reckon yourselves to be dead indeed to sin, but alive to God in Christ Jesus our Lord."

To be victorious in the cosmic conflict, we must accept that Christian life does not begin with birth, but death. Until self dies, until self is crucified, there is no beginning at all. There must be a radical, deliberate, total surgery of self. "Therefore, if anyone is in Christ, he is a new creation; old things have passed away; behold, all things have become new" (2 Corinthians 5:17).

Something happens to a person who lets Jesus become the full Controller of life. Simon the vacillator becomes Peter the valiant. Saul the marauder becomes Paul the martyr. Thomas the pessimist becomes the pioneer of the missionary frontier. Cowardice gives place to courage. Unbelief turns into a torch of faith. Jealousy is swallowed up by love. Self-interest vanishes into brotherly concern. Sin has no room in the heart. Self stands crucified.

The call of the Cross is a call to deny self its persistent desire to be its own Savior. It is a call to adhere fully to the Man of the cross, in order that our "faith might not rest in the wisdom of men but in the power of God" (1 Corinthians 2:5, RSV). Only as we deny self and abide in Christ can we be victorious in the great controversy.

He is risen!

The last great hope Satan had in gaining victory over Christ in the great controversy was in the tomb. The Roman seal, the Roman guards, and the watchful eyes of the religious leaders assured him that no one could break the tomb and create a story that Christ is risen. But the devil's hope was an outrageous one. For what right does the tomb, a place for sinners, have over the One "who committed no sin" (1 Peter 2:22)? Moreover, the voice of God was not at the command of Satan. The Son did not sin. He obeyed the Father's will and on the third day, God called His Son to come out of the tomb. Mission accomplished, the Savior arose victorious over sin and Satan.

"When Jesus was laid in the grave, Satan triumphed. He dared to hope that the Saviour would not take up His life again. He claimed the

Lord's body, and set his guard about the tomb, seeking to hold Christ a prisoner.... When he saw Christ come forth in triumph, he knew that his kingdom would have an end, and that he must finally die."[7]

Satan, however, is a tenacious fighter. He knew he was defeated on the cross. He also knew that the Resurrection had sealed and confirmed his defeat. Yet, he will continue his work of deception until he meets his destruction at the end-time judgment.

Since Calvary, Satan relentlessly leads the human mind to question the efficacy of the Cross and the historicity of the Resurrection. Even within the church, those that ought to be proclaiming these truths with certainty raise doubts concerning the Cross and the Resurrection. What easier way to thwart the purposes of God! Appeals to intellectual correctness and scientific truths are made to deny faith its role to grasp the reality of resurrection.

Jesus' words to Thomas, "Blessed are they that have not seen, and yet have believed" (John 20:29, KJV) give the lie to Satan. In the spiritual conflict the universe is engaged in, spiritual things are spiritually discerned. Genuine faith reaches beyond the tangible and the visible and grasps the fact that the One who said, "It is finished" is also the One who is risen!

> When the great controversy shall be ended . . . the plan of redemption having been completed, the character of God is revealed to all created intelligences. The precepts of His law are seen to be perfect and immutable. Then sin has made manifest its nature, Satan his character. Then the extermination of sin will vindicate God's love and establish His honor before a universe of beings who delight to do His will, and in whose heart is His law.[8]

It is in the risen Jesus that we have the final victory in the great controversy.

---

1. *The Desire of Ages*, pp. 686, 687.
2. *Ibid.*, p. 690.
3. *Steps to Christ*, p. 15.
4. *The Desire of Ages*, p. 762.
5. Swami Vivekananda, *Speeches and Writings*, 3rd ed. (Madras, India: G. A. Natesan, n.d.), 39.
6. *The Desire of Ages*, p. 25.
7. *Ibid.*, p. 782.
8. *Ibid.*, p. 764.

CHAPTER

11

The
War Within

We are in a war. Not the one fought with guns, tanks, and fighter-bombers. Not the one that makes you cross the oceans. Not the one that makes you shoot, maim, and kill. Not the one for your country or tribe or honor.

Our war is real. It involves not just time but eternity. We have adequate weapons. Our objectives are well-defined. Our victory is already assured, if we are on the Victor's side. Our war is spiritual. The apostle Paul states, "For we do not wrestle against flesh and blood, but against principalities, against powers, against the rulers of the darkness of this age, against spiritual hosts of wickedness in the heavenly places" (Ephesians 6:12).

Whatever the grand and cosmic issues of the great controversy, right now the unseen battle between Christ and Satan is fought for the allegiance of the human heart and mind—yours and mine.

> Many look on this conflict between Christ and Satan as having no special bearing on their own life; and for them it has little interest. But within the domain of every human heart this controversy is repeated. Never does one leave the ranks of evil for the service of God without encountering the assaults of Satan. The enticements which Christ resisted were those that we find it so difficult to withstand.[1]

The assaults of Satan today against God's people are real, as it was when our Savior walked this earth. True, Satan stands defeated at the Cross. The objective victory against Satan in the cosmic battle between righteousness and sin, between God and Satan, was won on the cross and confirmed by the empty tomb. Satan along with sin and death will be finally eliminated in God's final act of judgment in cleansing the earth and establishing the new heavens and a new earth. But who will populate the new earth? Who will be citizens of the eternal kingdom of God? That question is decided each day here on earth, as we make our choices to be on the side of God or Satan. While the victory of the Cross has vindicated God's character of love and justice and established the supremacy of God's law, that victory needs to be reflected in the choices we make.

The choice is never easy to make and maintain. For Satan stands ever ready to deceive us and draw us from the love and power of God. He fights for the mind of each person on earth, with his masterful, deceptive skills. The choice of Judas is one example of the victory Satan can win. The choice of Peter is an example of how Satan can be defeated in the personal struggle against evil. But the battle for our allegiance continues on a personal scale.

Judas: one who lost

The fall of Judas is a classic study of how one becomes a prey to Satan. Judas, so everyone thought, was the best of the lot—a patriot, ready to risk his life to break the foreign yoke; an organizational expert; a financial wizard; a man of gallant hopes, cool courage, and planned daring.

The road began so well for him. He was entrusted with much. Every opportunity for advancement was his. Patience bent low to be gentle with his failures; hope looked up to discover a glimmer of light against every darkening cloud that passed over his life; love labored for over three years to straighten out the crookedness in him, and to replace the spirit of divided loyalty with unambiguous response.

But Judas leaped into the abyss of treachery.

What went wrong? Was it lust of money, lure of position, impatience with the Master's methods? Was it to force the issue, to create a situation that would compel Jesus to launch a dramatic inaugural of the Messianic kingdom? Was it the desperate act of a disappointed follower?

The way of Satan is not that simple. Judas's failure began long before the ultimate act of betrayal of Christ's call. When Jesus fed the 5,000 with five loaves and two fishes, Judas was the first to grasp the political value of the miracle. Wasn't the ability to produce food enough to rally the hungry millions to Jesus' side and launch a political coup against the hated Romans? When Jesus denounced the attempt to make Him a king, and instead announced Himself the "Bread of Life," that was the beginning of the disenchantment of Judas: "[Judas's] hopes were high; His disappointment was bitter."[2] Judas was not on the same wavelength as Jesus. The kingdom of Judas was not the same as the kingdom of Jesus. Out of that collision betrayal was born.

Thus the roots of Judas's sin were found in the assertion of self over and against the claims of the One who called. Self dominated Judas so much that he could not see any possibility that he could be wrong. Arrogance, accusation, pride, avarice, and even betrayal seemed not at all inappropriate in the reaching of the goal that self had set for itself. Even discipleship was just an avenue to achieve self's relentless pursuit of its own glory by its own method. And in the process the true meaning and intent of following the Lord got slighted. Thus when a devout follower of Jesus chose to anoint His feet with a costly ointment, Judas denounced the act as a foolish waste, a sentimental stupidity (John 12:1-8). All Judas could see was money; all he could sense was the immediate, not the eternal. He was totally insensitive to the truth that life consists of more than the material, more than the tangible. Judas weighed life perpetually in terms of the cashbox he carried with him. But Jesus pointed out that true living is to be found in the alabaster box—in the breaking of it, so that symbolically its precious ointment fills the world with the fragrance of Christ's sacrificial love. Judas had no room for the Cross. And betrayal emerged.

Luke, in the beginning of his story, tells how Jesus prayed all night alone in the mountain before He chose His disciples, including Judas (Luke 6:12-16). And Jesus believed that the Twelve were God's gift to Him (John 17:6-9). As the only Judean in the band of the Twelve, was Judas really an answer to prayer? Did Jesus choose him and in the process risk His own life? Love always takes risks: we see it in Creation, in the Exodus, in the Incarnation, at the Cross, in ourselves. So is there any wonder that Jesus risked the kingdom through the unknown, the unpredictable, the undependable person that Judas was? The risk reveals on the one hand the immensity of divine love and grace, and on the other the profound hurt betrayal causes to that love.

But no analysis of Judas can be complete without those poignant words of the third Gospel: "Then Satan entered into Judas" (Luke 22:3, RSV). Treachery begins with that temptation: the soft and sweet whisper of Satan that we are our own masters, and that we need neither God nor human to chart the course of life. And treachery ends with that kiss of betrayal, denying the One who loves us most.

Yet Satan cannot enter an unwilling victim. A willful, deliberate rejection of a relationship precedes the act of betrayal. "Instead of walking in the light, Judas chose to retain his defects. Evil desires, revengeful passions, dark and sullen thoughts, were cherished, until Satan had full control of the man. Judas became a representative of the enemy of Christ."[3]

From Judas, spiritual defeat flashes its warning through history: the road to treachery passes by everyone's household, including those who are called. To be called into discipleship is one thing; to choose to bear the cross is another. Only that disciple is safe who looks beyond the lure of self to the Selfless One, the Man of Calvary.

Peter: down, but up again

In contrast to Judas, Peter stands as an example of the struggle of discipleship—the lure of Satan competing with the love of Christ, the potential for falling grappling with the triumph of faith.

The Gospels record two great confessions of Peter. First was Peter's confession that Jesus is the Christ, the Son of the living God (Matthew 16:16-20). Peter was among the first to accept the truth that Christ was God in human flesh. But immediately after that confession, when Jesus outlined that His mission involved His death, Peter chided Jesus that it shall not be so. Peter had his own vision of Messiahship, and that vision did not involve a cross, but a crown. Had he left his fishing net and the comforts of his home for a Person who would die?

Peter could not see the full picture of God's purpose, and saw only a kingdom of glory and power. Was he any different from Judas? He, too, in a way, acted as a tool of the devil in attempting to persuade Jesus to choose a path away from the Cross. When we deny God's way and choose other alternatives, we play the devil's game. And Jesus rebuked Peter with sharp words:

"Get behind Me, Satan! You are an offense to Me, for you are not mindful of the things of God, but the things of men." Then

The War Within

Jesus said to His disciples, "If anyone desires to come after Me, let him deny himself, and take up his cross, and follow Me" (Matthew 16:23, 24).

Peter learned that bitter lesson slowly. He began to understand, however dimly at that moment, that the kingdom of God involved the Cross, and his discipleship called for carrying his cross for the sake of Christ.

The second confession of Peter recorded in John 6:67-68 reveals twin aspects of discipleship. First: the continual admission that Christ is the Son of the living God. That confession is our ground to stand. Without submitting to Christ as God's Son sent for our salvation, discipleship does not even begin. The second aspect reveals complete self-abandonment to the call to discipleship: "Lord, to whom shall we go? You have the words of eternal life." For Peter, there were no alternatives to Jesus.

In such self-abandonment and absolute dependency on Christ, discipleship must rest. But the journey of discipleship has its ups and downs. Peter, human that he was, wavered again soon after the Last Supper. When Jesus revealed that He would soon die and the disciples would desert Him, Peter's impulsiveness was to affirm his self-confidence: whatever others might do, he would never deny his Lord. But the Lord knew better (Matthew 26:33-35).

The impetuous Peter could not stay awake for an hour in prayer for his Master in Gethsemane, but could draw his sword to fight for Him. Yet within hours, Satan seemed to have his hold on the disciple, and Peter denied ever knowing Jesus—not once but three times.

Discipleship never promises sinlessness. It is not a road without pitfalls. But it does provide assurance to the penitent. Peter fell to Satan's attack and denied his Lord. But the difference between Judas and Peter lay in what followed the denial. Judas committed suicide (defending his honor?) rather than repent of his egotistic pride. Peter repented with remorse and then returned to follow the Lord. "It was through self-sufficiency that Peter fell; and it was through repentance and humiliation that his feet were again established."[4] "In the whole Satanic force there is not power to overcome one soul who in simple trust casts himself on Christ."[5]

Where there is total commitment to the lordship of Jesus, there is perfect assurance. The divine Mediator provides us the same promise in our spiritual struggles that He gave to Peter: " 'Simon, Simon! Indeed,

Satan has asked for you, that he may sift you as wheat. But I have prayed for you, that your faith should not fail; and when you have returned to Me, strengthen your brethren' " (Luke 22:31, 32).

The warfare

The apostle Paul outlines the great warfare that engages the Christian:

> Finally, my brethren, be strong in the Lord and in the power of His might. Put on the whole armor of God, that you may be able to stand against the wiles of the devil. For we do not wrestle against flesh and blood, but against principalities, against powers, against the rulers of the darkness of this age, against spiritual hosts of wickedness in the heavenly places (Ephesians 6:10-12).

The word translated "finally" may well be rendered as "henceforth" or "from now on." The coming of Christ into history is thus a momentous breakthrough in history, making great spiritual victories possible. But the apostle does not wish the Christian to be unaware of the hidden dangers in the journey of faith. "From now on," he says there is a battle to be fought, there is a war to be won. Yes, Jesus fought and won the war against sin on Calvary, but from now on as we accept that provision and follow Him, the "wiles of the devil" are turned against us. The time between the Cross and the final end of this age is a time of agony and conflict for God's people.

Paul would have us remember certain vital points about this spiritual battle.

First, the war is not against flesh and blood. We are not involved in any struggle with any human beings. Christians are not to consider even the unbeliever as their enemy. Indeed, we are called to "live peaceably with all men" (Romans 12:18). We are to love all people alike, and tell them the good news of Jesus. No one for whom Christ died can be our opponent.

Second, we wrestle against spiritual forces of darkness. We are involved in a close, almost hand-to-hand combat with the evil forces at the head of which is Satan. The apostle identifies various characteristics of these forces. They are "the wiles of the devil." He may not attack openly, even though that is a definite possibility. But he is more sophisticated and may often appear as an "angel of light" (2 Corinthians 11:14). He is a dangerous wolf, but often chooses to disguise himself as a sheep that enters Christ's fold. Part of the cunning wiles of Satan is his successful attempt to subvert truth by lies and half-truths. The slogans of our age reflect such cunningness:

"God is what you make of him. All gods are the same."
"Truth is not absolute; it all depends . . ."
"There is no such thing as sin. There is only failure. There is behavioral aberration."
"We don't need a Savior; we need spirituality."
"Death is not real; it is a door to another life."
"There is no divine law governing human conduct; only socially accepted principles."
"Forget prayer; go for meditation."
"Grace is not a divine provision, but a human potential."

We can add to the litany of such slogans, dangled by Satan before our minds, hoping that we will fall prey to one or all. Every such notion has its seed of deception, but the end result of accepting such concepts is to deny the reality of God as He seeks our acceptance and discipleship. So Paul warns: "Stand against the wiles of the devil."

Third, we wrestle against evil forces that are supernatural and deadly. It is fashionable, both within and outside the church, to deny the existence of Satan and his cohorts. Nothing pleases the devil more. But no Christian is safe from his wily attack unless he recognizes both Satan's reality and his power. Satan knows the history of the human race. He knows you. And he intends to drag you down his path. No power can keep us from his wiles, unless we find our refuge in Him who overcame him on the cross. Hence Paul's counsel: "Put on the whole armor of God, that you may be able to stand against the wiles of the devil."

The weapons in the warfare

Paul underscores that the reality of Christian warfare is brought in three ways. First, he identifies the enemy as the supernatural force of darkness, who stands defeated by the Cross, and hence in full rage against Christ's disciples. Second, he counsels the believers to action as they face their warfare: Stand! Take up! Put on! Be strong! This is no time for vacillation. The battle is real. Third, he provides hope by urging the Christian to put on "the whole armor of God."

The emphasis on the "whole" should not be missed. The apostle lists at least six weapons that make up the armor. All are forged and furnished by God as one unit, and we cannot afford to neglect one without weakening the armor or making it of none effect.

The Christian is vulnerable at many spots, and often that characteristic, he thinks is his strongest turns out, under temptation, to be his weakest. As a chain is no stronger than its weakest link, so the Christian is no stronger than his weakest element of character. In view of the variety of foes that must be met and the various weaknesses of the flesh, nothing less than the entire armor will suffice.[6]

What are the various elements of this armor? We turn to Ephesians 6:13-17.

First, truth. A belt tied around the waist holds up one's clothing, and in the case of a soldier provides a slot to hold his sword. The soldier can march without any impediment. The Christian's belt is truth. Truth in the person of Jesus must envelop our entire being so that He holds up our tunic in times of warfare.

Second, the breastplate of righteousness. Christ our Righteousness—that is, the initiative that God has taken to provide us justification by faith—no doubt not only begins our redemptive experience, but frees us from condemnation. But justification is not an empty word. It calls for a change in life. A character that is morally weak cannot help in the battle against the devil.

Third, the shoes of the gospel of peace. The feet of a Christian are covered by the gospel of peace. Not only to proclaim the peace of the gospel but to show that in the midst of weary battles, the Christian's standing is on solid ground and he or she is at peace with God (Romans 5:1). Whatever battle is fought, no one can take away the peace that is part of the Christian life.

Fourth, the shield of faith. "This is the victory," wrote John, "that has overcome the world—our faith" (1 John 5:4). Faith in God is an invaluable treasure entrusted to a Christian. It is more than a passive trust in God and a quiet confidence in His leadership. It is active in that it is an armor with which one fights the evil one in the spiritual warfare.

Fifth, the helmet of salvation. The whole experience of salvation—God's saving power, His deliverance from the evil one, His forgiveness of sin, His adoption of us as His children—is our only defense against the enemy. Salvation includes the forgiveness of the past, the sanctification of the present, and the hope of ultimate reunion with the Savior.

Sixth, the sword of the Spirit which is the Word of God. While other parts of the armor are defensive, here we have an offensive weapon. The Word of God, inspired by the Holy Spirit, is the sword with which the Christian goes to battle. Jesus did it in the wilderness, and defeated Satan. So can we.

To all these parts of the armor, the apostle adds prayer at the end (Ephesians 6:18). Not as though prayer is unimportant, but precisely because it is important in the Christian warfare. In fact, Paul includes it as one imperative that must pervade the entire Christian preparation for the war. "Pray always," he says. A life of truth, righteousness, peace, faith, salvation, the Word, and a life soaked in prayer cannot but be victorious in the great battle fought within.

Who can be against us?

Our victory in the war within depends on whether we continually abide in Christ. Paul puts it more graphically: "I am crucified with Christ: nevertheless I live; yet not I, but Christ liveth in me: and the life which I now live in the flesh I live by faith of the Son of God, who loved me and gave himself for me" (Galatians 2:20).

Christian life recognizes not only the Crucifixion on Calvary, which is the basis of our salvation, but also the daily death of self. Self is the persistent tool of Satan: to exalt oneself, to affirm self-sufficiency, and thus put aside the need for continual abiding in Christ. On the other hand, Jesus said, "Abide in Me." That is the essence of Christian faith and living.

But the abiding is always in the present tense. We cannot take care of today by yesterday's abiding; nor can we deal with tomorrow by today's abiding. It must be a continual daily experience in order to claim and live Jesus' victory daily over the evil one. "Christ who lives *in* me" is the secret of overcoming self and Satan. Where He abides, there can be no competitor. And if He is for us, who can be against us?

---

1. *The Desire of Ages*, p.116.
2. *Ibid.*, p. 719.
3. *Ibid.*, p. 295.
4. *Christ's Object Lessons*, p. 155.
5. *Ibid.*, p. 157.
6. *The SDA Bible Commentary*, 6:1044.

The Great Controversy and the Church

With the Cross and the Resurrection, Satan's doom was sealed. However, the great controversy will not be over until this good news of salvation from sin and Satan's power is taken to the world at large. " 'This gospel of the kingdom will be preached,' " said Jesus, " 'in all the world as a witness to all the nations, and then the end will come' " (Matthew 24:14).

Jesus commissioned His disciples and through them the church with this work of taking the good news of the gospel to the world. However, from its very inception, the church has been hindered from spreading the joy of salvation by forces opposed to the gospel commission. These forces, under numerous guises, both within and outside the church, have plagued the church's attempt to spread the joy of salvation. Persecution, doctrinal corruption, disharmony, and neglect of the Word are some of what the enemy used to disrupt the church and its mission.

But Christ does not leave the church without any assistance. Through His Spirit and by remaining steadfast to the Word of God, the faithful continue their mission. History testifies to both the disruptive activities of Satan and the protective ministry of Christ with regard to the church and its work on this earth.[1]

The Great Controversy and the Church

Commission and power

One of the last acts of Jesus after the Resurrection was His commissioning the disciples to take the good news of His victory over sin and death to the entire world.

> "Go therefore and make disciples of all the nations, baptizing them in the name of the Father and of the Son and of the Holy Spirit, teaching them to observe all things that I have commanded you; and lo, I am with you always, even to the end of the age" (Matthew 28:19-20).

"This world is mine," boasts Satan. But with the victory of the Cross, Satan stands defeated in his claims. "I have overcome the world," says Christ. The victory of Christ brought about not only the defeat of Satan, but the assurance of salvation to all those who believe in Him. This is the good news. This is the gospel that Jesus wanted His disciples to take to all the nations. Go. Disciple. Baptize. Teach. These are the commands of the commission the church was charged with in the name of the Godhead.

Because of this urgent commission, the Christian can and must say: "The world is my parish." The theater of Satan's operation becomes the object of the believer's mission. The commission beckons every believer to become a witness to the gospel of joy.

The purpose of delivering the good news to the world is threefold: to bring sinners to the saving grace of God, to prepare a community of faith in which believers can fellowship with one another, and to make ready this community to meet their Savior when He returns. But Satan's intention is to keep people from ever knowing about God's forgiving love and to scatter the sheep away from the good Shepherd. To do this, he employs numerous ploys. He lets false teachers come in the church and teach doctrines that are contrary to God's Word. He rejoices in dividing the Christian community into different factions. He promotes a discipleship that makes no demands.

But the Lord who gave us redemption and who charged us with the commission to be His witnesses does not expect us to go at it alone. We are never alone in His vineyard. Along with the commission, Jesus gave assurance: " 'Lo, I am with you always' " (Matthew 28:20). That is a promise that cannot fail.

What did Jesus mean by this great promise with regard to His commission?

First, the commission is the task of Jesus. Even though Christ has laid the task of evangelism and witness on us as individual disciples and as a corporate body of believers, the work essentially remains His. We are to be His simple instruments to go, teach, baptize, and make disciples—not by our own power, but by His power. He has promised to be with us always even unto the end. Evangelism is neither failure nor success; it is witness, and the Lord who is always with us will care for it in His own way.

Second, Jesus is always our Eternal Contemporary. "I am" with you always, is the Lord's assurance. He is the great I AM. The One who tenderly cared for Adam and Eve in the Garden; the One who led Noah to the safety of the ark; the One who made His covenant with Abraham; the One who led the mighty Exodus movement to freedom; the One who gave the law to help humanity see His vision for the universe; the One who sent Isaiah, Jeremiah, Daniel, and all other prophets to proclaim and preserve His Word; the One who became flesh and died for us is the One who says, "Lo, I am with you."

Third, Jesus is the One who empowers us to fulfill the commission. " 'As the Father has sent Me, I also send you' " (John 20:21). Through the commission, He makes us a link in Heaven's rescue chain. The Father sent the Son. The Son sends us. What a privilege it is to be a witness and a bearer of the good news! Yet, we are not to do this ourselves. Jesus, before His ascension, told the disciples to "tarry" in Jerusalem for the power of the Holy Spirit (Luke 24:49). " 'You shall receive power when the Holy Spirit has come upon you; and you shall be witnesses to Me in Jerusalem, and in all Judea and Samaria, and to the end of the earth' " (Acts 1:8).

It is through the Holy Spirit that Jesus is always with us. In His name and in the power of the Spirit, we must carry out the commission. Like the apostles did at the Pentecost, when one sermon resulted in 3,000 baptisms (Acts 2:41). The apostolic church did it. So can we.

Early struggles

The Jewish leaders had supposed that the work of Christ would end with His death; but, instead of this, they witnessed the marvelous scenes of the Day of Pentecost. They heard the disciples, endowed with a power and energy hitherto unknown, preaching Christ, their words confirmed by signs and wonders.[2]

This success brought about by the Holy Spirit greatly angered Satan and his earthly agents. Satan used everything in his power to halt the progress of the gospel. And so he launched a torrent of oppression against the apostles and the believers. The attack took various forms: persecution, dishonesty, murmuring within the church, and even death. But crisis can bring the best or worst in humans. Because the apostles relied upon the Spirit, every crisis was turned into an opportunity for greater witness. Every persecution brought more people to accept Jesus (Acts 4:4; 5:14-16).

Perhaps the most threatening battle Satan launched against the early church was the stoning of Stephen (Acts 7). Satan expected that the public lynching of a man "full of faith and the Holy Spirit" (Acts 6:5) would crush the spirit of the early church and send it into oblivion. But the Holy Spirit used Stephen to turn the occasion of his death into a pulpit for proclamation. Stephen's sermon was not only a revelation of God's truth from the early times of the Old Testament to the death and the Resurrection, but also a proclamation that Jesus is the fulfillment of the Scriptures and is the coming King. From the temple on earth to the temple in heaven, Stephen erected a verbal ladder and invited his hearers to see the risen Jesus seated on the Father's throne.

> The martyrdom of Stephen made a deep impression upon all who witnessed it. The memory of the signet of God upon his face; his words, which touched the very souls of those who heard them, remained in the minds of the beholders, and testified to the truth of that which he had proclaimed. His death was a sore trial to the church, but it resulted in the conviction of Saul, who could not efface from his memory the faith and constancy of the martyr, and the glory that had rested on his countenance.[3]

The blood of martyrs, it is said, is the seed of the church. Stephen's death did not crush the church, as Satan expected. Instead, it shocked many in Jerusalem who were led to examine the scriptural testimony to

Jesus that Stephen so eloquently outlined. And many became believers. One whose soul was convicted was Saul of Tarsus who later became the apostle who shook the world for the gospel.

The parallel in history cannot be missed. Whenever and wherever the church was persecuted, there has been the largest growth, sometimes silently, sometimes publicly. Be it in India or in China or Russia or any other place, persecution never silences the witness of the truth.

Early victories

Struggles and victories of the apostolic church form the theme of the book of Acts. In spite of Satan's warring attempts to destroy or disillusion the church, the Holy Spirit worked on the hearts and minds of believers to preserve the church's faithfulness and to persevere in obeying the Great Commission.

Throughout the history of the church Satan has tried to scuttle the onward progress of God's work in the cosmic conflict. Satan may have succeeded to some extent, but God always has His faithful ones. Through them, God has kept the torch of truth ever burning, and His witness never fading. The first few chapters of Acts show the secret of the apostolic success. In spite of all that Satan could do, those valiant early believers affirmed their standing ground in the Scriptures and made bold their declaration of truths that are vital to gospel proclamation and essential for victory in the great controversy. Here are some of those affirmations that can be forgotten only to the peril of our mission:

- Christ is both divine and human; that He is God-Incarnate and is the basis of all our beliefs (Acts 2:36).
- The Bible and the Bible only ought to be the basis of our faith and preaching. (Count the number of Old Testament quotations found in (Acts 1–4.)
- Unity is vital to Christian life and proclamation (Acts 2:46).
- Christianity is a life of stewardship, not hoarding (Acts 4:32-37).
- Christian life is submission to the Holy Spirit (Acts 2–5).
- Christian courage is born from obedience to God (Acts 5:29).
- The church needs a structure and a mission (Acts 6; 12).

- The kingdom of God is a family without walls (Acts 10).
- The problems of the church are to be solved by a consensus of the church leaders under the guidance of the Holy Spirit (Acts 15).

Would all these and more have become possible without the tender care and regard of the risen Jesus to His church? Upon these victories, God has built the family of God. And even today as we struggle with the issues of the cosmic conflict, working against the wiles of Satan, our safety lies in the truth as it is in Jesus and as revealed in the Scriptures.

Corrupting the truth

The apostolic church was not without dangers from within and without. Even as it pursued its mission, there were already attacks on the purity of the gospel truth, and the apostles had to resist each one of them through the power of the Holy Spirit.

Paul warned early in his ministry: " 'For I know this, that after my departure savage wolves will come in among you, not sparing the flock. Also from among yourselves men will rise up, speaking perverse things, to draw away the disciples after themselves' " (Acts 20:29, 30).

John was even more particular about the corruption that was already taking place in his time:

> Little children, it is the last hour; and as you have heard that the Antichrist is coming, even now many antichrists have come, by which we know that it is the last hour. They went out from us, but they were not of us; for if they had been of us, they would have continued with us; but they went out that they might be made manifest, that none of them were of us (1 John 2:18, 19).

Notice the tender words of John: "They went out from us, they were not of us." False doctrines do not necessarily enter the church from outside, but from within, from those who have not fully accepted the Word of God. Where there is a lack of total commitment to Christ and His revelation of God, and where there is a lack of faithful acceptance of

God's Word, and where self raises its head to affirm its own theories, false doctrines enter the church and corrupt the mission and the ministry for which the church exists.

> By the pride of human wisdom, by contempt for the influence of the Holy Spirit, and by disrelish for the truths of God's word, many who profess to be Christians, and who feel competent to teach others, will be led to turn away from the requirements of God.[4]

How true this is as we survey the history of the church. Between the close of the apostolic age and the Reformation, Satanic influence on Christianity led to divisions, false doctrines, and persecutions. Either the influence of Roman and Greek philosophies or the desire for power and self-exaltation on the part of various church centers in the vast Roman Empire, gradually led the church to apostasy. Some of the false doctrines that came into the church are:

- The immortality of the soul; ever-burning hell; purgatory.
- Infant baptism.
- Mariolatry (worship of Mary, Jesus' mother).
- Mediation through saints.
- Attempt to change the law of God; observance of Sunday sabbath.
- Righteousness by works as opposed to righteousness by faith.
- Church tradition preferred over the Bible; taking away the Bible from common people.
- Pope as the vicar of Christ, with spiritual and doctrinal authority; papal infallibility.

The nominal conversion of Constantine in the early part of the fourth century caused Christianity to loose even more of its purity. This event caused rejoicing throughout Christendom, but the world, cloaked in false righteousness, walked into the church. The corruption of truth progressed. Paganism became the victor. Although wearing now the garb of Christianity, its false doctrines, ceremonies, superstitions, and traditions became part of Christian faith and worship. This "gigantic system of false religion is a masterpiece of Satan's power—a monument of his efforts to seat himself upon the throne to rule the earth according to his will."[5]

But not forever.

Back to the Bible

Historians call it the Middle or Dark Ages, a period of about twelve centuries stretching until the time of the great Protestant Reformation. For the secular historians, it was a period of intellectual darkness, when the traditions of the church ruled supreme. But for those who understand history as part of the flow of the great controversy, it was a period in which the light of the gospel was minimized and made subject to the whim and fancy of human tradition and church practices. These were based not on the Word of God, but the authority of human powers. It was an era of spiritual darkness.

> The darkness seemed to grow more dense . . . The most absurd and superstitious customs prevailed. The minds of men were so completely controlled by superstition that reason itself seemed to have lost its sway. While priests and bishops were themselves pleasure-loving, sensual, and corrupt, it could only be expected that the people who looked to them for guidance would be sunken in ignorance and vice.[6]

One of the primary efforts of Satan to keep people in spiritual ignorance in the Middle Ages was to suppress the Word of God. Bible study was confined to monks in the monasteries. The ordinary Christian had no access to the lamp and light of life. In fact, it was unlawful for ordinary church members to have Bibles. But God in His own miraculous way intervened, and he used the effort of the Englishman John Wycliffe to translate the Bible into the language of his people. The stage was set for Reformation. "In giving the Bible to his countrymen, he had done more to break the fetters of ignorance and vice, more to liberate and elevate his country, than was ever achieved by the most brilliant victories on fields of battle."[7]

But the deadly blow to spiritual apostasy came through the pen and voice of Martin Luther. A monk himself, he sought inward peace, resisted human traditions, and turned to the Word for God's guidance.

There he found two great truths, long neglected by the official church of the time. The first was the Bible. The more he read it, the more the Holy Spirit convinced him that there was no other way to truth except the Bible and the Bible only. Christians ought to obey the Word and not human traditions. He took

> . . . a solemn vow to study carefully and to preach with fidelity the word of God, not the sayings and doctrines of the popes, all the days of his life. He was no longer the mere monk or professor, but the authorized herald of the Bible. He had been called as a shepherd to feed the flock of God, that were hungering and thirsting for the truth. He firmly declared that Christians should receive no other doctrines than those which rest on the authority of the Sacred Scriptures. These words struck at the very foundation of papal supremacy. They contained the vital principle of the Reformation.[8]

With his conscience subject to the Bible and his study exploring its precious truths, he found the second important truth of the Reformation: the just shall live by faith. The study of Romans and Galatians led Luther to discover that salvation does not come by human merits. Salvation is the gracious work of Christ, to be received in faith. The good news of the gospel is that it is the power of God unto salvation to those who believe in Jesus. Human works have no role to play in justification. This precious truth brought Luther inner peace and true reconciliation with God.

Until Luther preached that the just shall live by faith alone, the Roman Church had taught that a person could be saved by following its traditions, and that forgiveness of sin can even be obtained by the purchase of indulgences. Luther denounced such traditional beliefs and proclaimed

> . . . that it is impossible for man, by his own works, to lessen its guilt or evade its punishment. Nothing but repentance toward God and faith in Christ can save the sinner. The grace of Christ cannot be purchased; it is a free gift. He counseled the people not to buy indulgences, but to look in faith to a crucified Redeemer.[9]

The Great Controversy and the Church

The road to fuller understanding of the Bible and its great truths was set. Soon other Reformers, such as Calvin, Zwingli, Melanchthon, and Wesley rose to restore the lost biblical teachings. As a result, the emerging Protestant church rejected such falsehoods as purgatory, indulgences, prayers for the dead, transubstantiation (the belief that the bread and wine of the Communion actually becomes the flesh and blood of Jesus), mediation of saints, and various other practices that had no biblical foundation.

The work of the Reformers was not easy. Unseen forces led by Satan attempted to crush this return to the Bible.

> God's faithful servants were not toiling alone. While principalities and powers and wicked spirits in high places were leagued against them, the Lord did not forsake His people. Could their eyes have been opened, they would have seen as marked evidence of divine presence and aid as was granted to a prophet [Elisha] of old . . .Thus did angels guard the workers in the cause of the Reformation.[10]

The Reformation, however, did not restore such truths as Sabbath, the state of the dead, and Jesus' high priestly ministry. But it did advance the cause of Christ in the great controversy and prepared the way for the whole truth to be revealed to the world. That would be the task of the Seventh-day Adventist Church that arose from the Millerite movement (1839-1844).

---

1. For a full and detail account of the conflict between Christ and Satan played out in the history of the church, read *Great Controversy*, chapters 1-20.

2. *Ibid.*, p. 44

3. *Ibid.*, p. 101.

4. *Ibid.*, p. 504.

5. *The Great Controversy*, p. 50.

6. *Ibid.*, p. 57.

7. *Ibid.*, p. 88.

8. *Ibid.*, p. 125.

9. *Ibid.*, p. 129.

10. *Ibid.*, p. 173.

CHAPTER 13

The End
of the Controversy

The first book of the Bible tells us how the great controversy began on earth. The last book tells how it will end in the triumph of God and the destruction of Satan. In between, the pages of the Bible are filled with how the great controversy began, and how the cosmic battle between God and Satan has occupied the redemptive history of humankind. Sacred history is the narration of the contours of this conflict:

> In the word of God the curtain is drawn aside, and we behold, behind, above, and through all the play and counterplay of human interests and power and passions, the agencies of the all-merciful One, silently, patiently working out the counsels of His own will.[1]

In our study so far, we have seen from the Bible what the issues of the great controversy are, how Satan attempts to deceive human beings, how God through Christ has provided a way of overcoming Satan's assaults and sin's power, and how we as individuals are to fight our own battles. We have also seen how Christ triumphed over Satan on the cross and assured victory in the great controversy. But how will the conflict ultimately end?

The book of Revelation gives us some answers. Revelation 12:17 tells us that Satan is planning one last battle before the end of the great controversy: "And the dragon was wroth with the woman, and went to make war with the remnant of her seed, which keep the commandments of God, and have the testimony of Jesus Christ."

Satan's last attack

The Scriptures at times uses "woman" to represent the church. A corrupt woman represents the apostatized church. Here in Revelation 12, the prophet pictures the struggle of the true church, which will culminate with the final attack of Satan on the "remnant" of her seed, which is identified as a group of people that will "keep the commandments of God and have the testimony of Christ."

Seventh-day Adventists, from their beginning in the middle of the nineteenth century, have identified themselves as this remnant. Such identification was not born out of any ecclesiastical monopoly or spiritual arrogance, but out of their recognition that they were called in the end time as a special people to complete the task of the Reformation and restore truth in all its fullness.

A major part of this restoration of truth is the call to "keep the commandments of God"—the entire law including the Sabbath. While they submit to the Word fully and unreservedly in teaching and in conduct, and while they accept righteousness by faith as the only way of salvation, they are fully aware of the demand the Word makes upon the redeemed believer: obedience to all the commandments of God. Their insistence on Sabbath is nothing more than following Jesus who kept the Sabbath law "as his custom was" (Luke 4:16), and following the apostles who so faithfully kept the Sabbath in the early church.

While claiming to be the remnant church, Adventists

. . . repudiate emphatically and unequivocally any thought that they alone are children of God and have a claim upon heaven. They believe that all who worship God in full sincerity, that is, in terms of all the revealed will of God that they understand, are presently potential members of that final 'remnant' company . . . Adventists believe that it is their solemn privilege to make God's last testing truths so clear and so persuasive as to draw all of God's children into that prophetically foretold company that is making ready for the day of God.[2]

That company—the remnant church—is identified as one that will keep the commandments of God and have the testimony of Jesus. Because of this, the dragon is enraged and will let loose the final struggle against them in the last stages of the cosmic conflict. Adventists have understood this final struggle as one that will concentrate on their unconditional insistence on obedience as part of faithful discipleship.

> The warfare against God's law, which was begun in heaven, will be continued until the end of time. Every man will be tested. Obedience or disobedience is the question to be decided by the whole world. All will be called to choose between the law of God and the laws of men. Here the dividing line will be drawn. There will be but two classes. Every character will be fully developed; and all will show whether they have chosen the side of loyalty or that of rebellion.[3]

Adventists also hold that Sabbath will be a particular test point in the final conflict:

> The Sabbath will be the great test of loyalty, for it is the point of truth especially controverted. When the final test shall be brought to bear upon men, then the line of distinction will be drawn between those who serve God and those who serve Him not. While the observance of the false sabbath in compliance with the law of the state, contrary to the fourth commandment, will be an avowal of allegiance to a power that is in opposition to God, the keeping of the true Sabbath, in obedience to God's law, is an evidence of loyalty to the Creator.[4]

Since the law was at the core of the great controversy as it unfolded in heaven, and since the remnant church calls upon all the people to obey the law of God, is it any wonder that Satan is in rage against the church and will wish to destroy it? In his attempt, he will receive assistance from religio-political powers, a state-religion combined with unusual powers, who will unleash all their energy to destroy the remnant church.[5]

Even as the clouds of that final conflict gather over, as time rushes to its end, as the coming of Jesus draws hear, the remnant church has a mission to perform: the proclamation of heaven's three-fold warning to a world in rebellion, found in Revelation 14:6-12.

The first message

God's final warning message to this world is proclaimed by three angels. Since the gospel commission is specifically given to God's people (Matthew 28:19), "angels" must refer to God's saints engaged in the task of proclaiming the gospel. The angels are said to fly "in the midst of heaven." That is to say, their message is meant for the entire world. It includes Hindus, Moslems, Buddhists, atheists, and all those who do not have a full knowledge of the gospel. It includes everybody. The church that proclaims this message, therefore, cannot afford to erect any walls around themselves. It needs to be open, reaching out: global in mission and purpose, united by one common message and direction. The prophet describes the message as the "everlasting gospel." The same gospel that was planned out before the foundations of this earth were laid. The same gospel that was preached to Adam. The same gospel that saved Noah. The same gospel that was revealed to Abraham. The same gospel that Moses displayed through the sanctuary system. The same gospel that the apostles preached.

The angel spells out the everlasting gospel? " 'Fear God and give glory to Him, for the hour of His judgment has come; and worship Him who made heaven and earth, the sea and springs of water' " (Revelation 14:7). If this is the same gospel as was preached through the ages, in what sense is there now a need for this special end-time proclamation? Two points that have a bearing on the great controversy need to be stressed.

First, the priority of God in life. "Fear God and give glory to Him." Our reverence and glory are forever to be reserved for the Creator. This is a holy ground, and there should be no competitor. Often we forget that. We do not sense our daily, moment-by-moment need for God. We look at Him as sort of a fireman—to be called upon whenever there is a fire. No, the everlasting gospel is the good news of a God who ever lives and demands of us first priority.

But that's not all. The message of "fear God and give glory to Him" is proclaimed in the context of an end-time event. "For the hour of His judgment has come." God's judgment implies the time of reckoning as to what we have done with His law, and the provision He has made for the transgression of that law. We will be judged by His law—the same law that Satan accused in heaven as being arbitrary and unjust. The end of the great controversy cannot really be an end unless the fairness and the uprightness and the eternal nature of the law is established.

Because of the certainty of the judgment, we are called upon to fear God and give glory to Him.

The second and equally important reason for the newness of the "everlasting gospel" is in the second part of the message: "Worship Him who made heaven and earth, the sea and springs of water." As we have seen early in this book, one of the crucial issues in the great controversy is worship. Worship is God's prerogative, and He expects all creatures to worship Him. But Satan in his selfish pride sought worship for himself. The final message to the world warns again that as we near the end Satan will minimize the need to worship God and in its place substitute other gods: self, materialism, secularism, New Age, humanism, or whatever. Anything that comes between an individual and God and prevents true worship is taking away the allegiance due only to God.

Moreover, the call to worship makes another specific demand: "worship Him who made heaven and earth." Worship of the Creator implies acknowledgment of God as the Creator. In an age that denies the creation of God, at a time where even Christians, good Christians, are ready to compromise on the doctrine of Creation as outlined in Genesis and deny its essential core, we are called upon to worship the Creator. Denial of Creation is playing into the hands of the devil.

How do we acknowledge God as the Creator? By worshiping Him, yes. The Bible, however, has prescribed a special way whereby we remember His creative power. Says the fourth commandment: " 'Remember the Sabbath day, to keep it holy. . . . For in six days the Lord made the heavens and the earth, the sea, and all that is in them, and rested the seventh day. Therefore the Lord blessed the Sabbath day and hallowed it' " (Exodus 20:8-11).

The End of the Controversy

Is it any wonder then, as the great controversy nears its ultimate end, that the final warning message of the three angels calls for the worship of the Creator and for honoring Him by honoring the Sabbath? Indeed Sabbath will be a crucial test of faithfulness in the final conflict.

The second message

"And another angel followed, saying, 'Babylon is fallen, is fallen, that great city, because she has made all nations drink of the wine of the wrath of her fornication'" (Revelation 14:8). Babylon is symbolic of disbelief in God and opposition to His truth. Lucifer is compared to the king of Babylon. God revealed to Nebuchadnezzar through the vision of the metallic image that the head of gold symbolized his kingdom of Babylon. But after him there would be another kingdom. So Nebuchadnezzar showed his defiance against God's revelation by building an image of all gold and commanding the empire to bow to it (Daniel 3).

Babylon in biblical imagery is apostasy. Any apostate system, secular or religious, and all false religious institutions and its leaders are included under the figurative term Babylon.

The second angel's message pronounces the doom of Babylon. In the final conflict, God's judgment will fall upon apostasy, as God prepares to cleanse this earth from all its impurities and set up His kingdom. Hence, the call issued by the angel: "Come out of Babylon." Her apostasy is great, and she has misled the entire world through one system or the other.

God is calling His people to come out of these apostate forces. They have rejected Christ and the salvation that comes through Him by faith and have led the world into all kinds of falsehood, including rejection of God's law and the Sabbath and belief in doctrines that are unscriptural.

The conflict between apostasy and truth will be so focused and so severe that the apostate forces will join together and try to destroy God's servants who are true to Him.

The powers of earth, uniting to war against the commandments of God, will decree that "all, both small and great, rich and poor, free and bond" (Revelation 13:16), shall conform to the customs of the church by the observance of the false sabbath. All who refuse compliance will be visited with civil penalties, and it will finally be declared that they are deserving of death.[6]

But at the end the judgment of God will fall on Babylon, and God will intervene to save those who remain loyal to Him. The judgments of God are sure and His promise is certain.

Third message

The third angel's message is connected with the first two:

> "If anyone worships the beast and his image, and receives his mark on his forehead or on his hand, he himself shall also drink of the wine of the wrath of God, which is poured out full strength into the cup of His indignation. He shall be tormented with fire and brimstone in the presence of the holy angels and in the presence of the Lamb. And the smoke of their torment ascends forever and ever; and they have no rest day or night, who worship the beast and his image, and whoever receives the mark of his name" (Revelation 14:9-11).

The beast and the image are undoubtedly the powers described in Revelation 13.[7] The beast is best noted for the work it is devoted to do: "to blaspheme His [God's] name, His tabernacle, and those who dwell in heaven . . . to make war with the saints and to overcome them." (Revelation 13:6, 7). The work of the image is to advance the cause of the beast (Revelation 13:11-16). Both the beast and image are thus apostate forces and institutions and their leaders, both secular and religious, that join together as we near the end time to oppose God's saints who remain loyal to truth. Under their power and influence

> . . . conscientious obedience to the word of God will be treated as rebellion. Blinded by Satan, the parent will exercise harshness and severity toward the believing child; the master or mistress will oppress the commandment-keeping servant. Affection will be alienated; children will be disinherited and driven from home . . . As the defenders of truth refuse to honor the

Sunday-sabbath, some of them will be thrust into prison, some will be exiled, some will be treated as slaves.[8]

Such will be fierceness of the last struggle. Against that coming crisis, the remnant church is called upon to proclaim the message of the three angels. That message is one of final victory. For the third angel concludes that all the apostate forces will stand crushed by God's ultimate judgment. But God's people are asked to wait for the final deliverance: "Here is the patience of the saints; here are those who keep the commandments of God and the faith of Jesus" (Revelation 14:12).

The next scene that John sees is that of the Son of man coming down from heaven on a white cloud with a sickle in His hand. The harvest is ripe. The judgment will fall on the apostate forces and their master, Satan.

The grand finale

As the final message of the three angels, faithfully proclaimed by God's saints, heads toward its climax, the closing events of earth's history will rapidly, suddenly, and surely, bring the great controversy to its ultimate end. Three significant events mark in no uncertain terms the doom of the devil and the reward of God's saints as they are taken home at last.

First, the return of Christ. Jesus promised He would return to take His children home " 'that where I am, there you may be also' " (John 14:3). At the time of His return, the living sinners are slain (2 Thessalonians 1:7-11). The living saints are translated and the righteous dead are resurrected. Together they ascend to meet the Lord in the air (1 Corinthians 15:51-55; 1 Thessalonians 4:16-18), immortalized and victorious over death (Revelation 20:6). This first resurrection in itself nails the first lie of Satan—"You shall not die." But Jesus has shown that sin results in death; His grace brings resurrection. Upon His return, He takes the saints, the living and resurrected ones, to heaven to be with Him during the millennium.

Second, Satan is bound here on earth for 1,000 years (Revelation 20:2). How is Satan bound? What does he do during this imprisonment?

Limited to the earth, he will not have access to other worlds to tempt and annoy those who have never fallen. It is in this sense that he is bound: there are none remaining, upon whom he can exercise his power. He is wholly cut off from the work of deception and ruin which for so many centuries has been his sole delight.[9]

What will the saints do with Christ for the thousand years? (Revelation 20:4). It is at that time the words of the apostle Paul will come true that we will judge the angels who are fallen (1 Corinthians 6:2, 3).

Since probation closes just before the second coming of Christ, this judgment will not decide anyone's salvation. It will review for the sake of the redeemed and the unfallen beings the rebellion of Satan and the fairness with which the wicked have been excluded from the family of God. At last, the time has come for the unfallen and the saved to understand the nature of Satan:

> Satan's rebellion was to be a lesson to the universe through all coming ages—a perpetual testimony to the nature of sin and its terrible results. The working out of Satan's rule, its effects upon both men and angels, would show what must be the fruit of setting aside the divine authority.[10]

Third, the final judgment. At the end of the millennium, John sees the Holy City, the New Jerusalem, descend from heaven to earth. In it are Christ and the redeemed (Revelation 21:2, 10). Christ resurrects the wicked to face their final judgment (Revelation 20:5). The return of all humanity (saints in the city, the wicked outside) triggers one final thought in Satan's diabolic mind, one grand scheme. He deceives the wicked to join him in an attack against the Holy City, but "fire came down from God out of heaven and devoured them. The devil . . . was cast into the lake of fire" (Revelation 20:9, 10).

But before the final end, one great acknowledgment will be made by all, including Satan. Before Jesus, the conquering hero, the King of kings and Lord of lords ". . . every knee should bow, of those in heaven, and of those on earth, and of those under the earth, and that every tongue should confess that Jesus Christ is Lord, to the glory of God the Father" (Philippians 2:10,11).

With the destruction of Satan and his followers, the war that began in heaven is finally over. The moral conflict is resolved. The earth itself is

126

renewed and purified by the fires that burn the wicked. The new earth becomes the home of the redeemed, with God Himself making His dwelling there (Revelation 21:1-4).

Heaven joins earth in a resounding praise to the works of God.

"Great and marvelous are Your works, Lord God Almighty! Just and true are Your ways, O King of the saints! Who shall not fear You, O Lord, and glorify Your name? For You alone are holy. For all nations shall come and worship before You, for Your judgments have been manifested" (Revelation 15:3, 4).

The great controversy is ended. Sin and sinners are no more. The entire universe is clean. One pulse of harmony and gladness beats through the vast creation. From Him who created all, flow life and light and gladness, throughout the realms of illimitable space. From the minutest atom to the greatest world, all things, animate and inanimate, in their unshadowed beauty and perfect joy, declare that God is love.[11]

---

1. *Education,* p. 173.

2. *The SDA Bible Commentary,* 7:815.

3. *The Desire of Ages,* p. 763.

4. *The Great Controversy,* p. 605.

5. The prophetic basis upon which Adventists arrive at this conclusion, see *The SDA Bible Commentary,* on Revelation 13.

6. *Ibid.,* p. 604.

7. For detailed information on the identity and work of the beast and image, see *The SDA Commentary,* on Revelation 13.

8. *The Great Controversy,* p. 608.

9. *Ibid.,* p. 689.

10. *Patriarchs and Prophets,* pp. 42, 43.

11. *The Great Controversy,* p. 678.

If you enjoyed this book, you'll enjoy these as well:

Knowing God in the Real World
Jon Paulien. Is the gospel still relevant in the 21st century? Paulien clarifies the basics of the gospel message, and demonstrates how that message can be expressed in a way that makes sense in the secular world.
0-8163-1812-3. Paperback. US$12.99, Cdn$19.49.

Shades of Grace
Ty Gibson. **Shades of Grace** is a series of penetrations into the mind and emotions of God. You will discover that His grace, far from being a sterile legal provision, is the outpouring of a divine love that will not let us go at any cost to Himself.
0-8163-1852-2. Paperback. US$12.99, Cdn$19.49.

The Gift
An unforgettable look at the sacrifice of Christ. *The Gift,* by Kim Allan Johnson, will put you back in touch with the God who would rather go to hell for you than to live in heaven without you.
0-8163-1768-2. Paperback. US$11.99, Cdn$17.99

Order from your ABC by calling **1-800-765-6955**, or get online and shop our virtual store at <u>www.adventistbookcenter.com</u>.

- Read a chapter from your favorite book
- Order online
- Sign up for email notices on new products